The Reception Year in Action

Children thrive when a reception class is organised and managed by the adults, but led by the children. They learn and develop if they are in a stimulating environment which is carefully organised and when observations are used to support their 'next steps'. They take risks and surpass expectations when they have clear routines and boundaries, combined with a supportive staff and an enabling environment.

The Reception Year in Action offers a unique insight into the workings of a highly successful Reception class as it progresses through a complete academic year. The book covers all aspects of practice from the organisation of the classroom and garden and the rationale behind this, to the routines and boundaries that ensure children are safe, happy and therefore able to explore and learn. It tracks the events of each month in the year, paying particular attention to the environment, the role of the adult, links with parents, children's individual needs and the key areas of learning and development. At each stage Anna Ephgrave gives the reason behind each decision and shows what the outcomes have been for the children.

This revised edition has been updated to show how the methods described complement the revised Early Years Foundation Stage framework and how the planning system has been received under the new OFSTED framework. Key features include:

- photocopiable pages of planning sheets, record keeping sheets, sample letters to parents and role play resources also available for download from www.routledge.com/9780415659734;
- over 150 full-colour photographs to illustrate practice;
- lists of resources and materials;
- examples of recorded observations and planning for next steps;
- guidance on what to look for when assessing children's progress.

Written by an advanced skills teacher who is gaining national recognition for her practice, this book provides teachers with the practical ideas and evidence of success to work with confidence in a way that is rewarding, manageable and, above all, best for the children.

Anna Ephgrave is Foundation Stage Co-ordinator at De Bohun School, nationally accredited Moderator for the London Borough of Enfield and an Advanced Skills Teacher with responsibility for the development of outdoor play in schools.

The Reception Year in Action

A month-by-month guide to success in the classroom

Revised and updated edition

Anna Ephgrave

Foreword by Helen Bilton

Routledge
Taylor & Francis Group

LONDON AND NEW YORK

Revised edition published 2013
by Routledge
2 Park Square, Milton Park, Abingdon, Oxon OX14 4RN

Simultaneously published in the USA and Canada
by Routledge
711 Third Avenue, New York, NY 10017

Routledge is an imprint of the Taylor & Francis Group, an informa business

First edition published by Routledge 2011

British Library Cataloguing in Publication Data
A catalogue record for this book is available from the British Library

Library of Congress Cataloging in Publication Data
Ephgrave, Anna.
The reception year in action : a month-by-month guide to success in the classroom / Anna Ephgrave. – Rev. and updated.
p. cm.
ISBN 978-0-415-65973-4 (pbk.) – ISBN 978-0-203-07358-2 (ebook) 1. Academic achievement–United States. 2. Education–Parent participation. 3. Student participation in curriculum planning–United States. 4. Home and school–United States. 5. Community and school. I. Title.
LB1062.6.E65 2012
371.20973–dc23
2012026866

ISBN: 978-0-415-65973-4 (pbk)
ISBN: 978-0-203-07358-2 (ebk)

Typeset in Bembo
by FiSH Books Ltd, Enfield

Printed and bound in Great Britain by the MPG Books Group

Contents

List of figures

Foreword

I had the great pleasure of being introduced to Anna Ephgrave and her practice in 2009. Everything I believe in was happening in her class and garden, it was a joy to behold.

Children were engaged in a range of activities from being footballers to builders, from dragons to babies. They were completely absorbed in what they were doing, but aware their play could take any turn as the staff and environment would facilitate and support them. Staff talked and listened to children and were quite clearly enjoying their work. There were discussions about height, weight, reach, time, success, quantity, emotions, possibilities. The conversations were real, involving sympathetic questioning to help children achieve their plans and ideas. It even rained a couple of times and this was a time to come together under the canopy and have a discussion about what next, or to just pick up a coat or umbrella and continue with the play. The children were learning so much and all the while they were keeping healthy.

Inside and out were one, the two spaces just merged. And if a child needed something from inside they went and got it and if they needed something from outside they did likewise. Children were not arguing and squabbling, they were getting on with the joy of being a child. What I particularly loved was the sense of unknown. We did not know where the day would go, or exactly what learning would happen but there was a sense of excitement and eager anticipation throughout the day.

This book describes very clearly that practice. It covers a year in the life of De Bohun reception class. Each chapter covers one month and has sections about the organisation and the environment and then a diary of events for that month. Every possible topic you can imagine from school dinners to weapon play, from attachment disorder to children using phonics to write, from Ferre Laevers levels of involvement to a visit to the florist are covered! It is a very accessible read and is almost addictive in its nature as you become fully immersed in the class of children and their development. What is particularly impressive about the practice is that so much happens outside right throughout the year.

Good quality early years practice is highly effective in helping children learn and develop emotionally, socially, physically, cognitively and linguistically, but it is hard to understand. This book makes understanding that unique early years approach very easy. This book will take the understanding of outdoor play, teaching and learning to a new level. Everyone who is involved with early years education and care should read this book!

Helen Bilton
PGCE Primary Programme Director, University of Reading

Acknowledgements

First of all I must thank my husband, Michael, who has given me encouragement and support over the past 18 months to ensure that I finished this book. The initial idea for the text came from Helen Bilton and I wish to thank her for believing that I had something to offer other practitioners. Ruth Moore, our Early Years Strategy Manager, has also given me the confidence and back-up to explore new possibilities in school.

Of course, the events described in the book would not have been possible without a wonderful team and a supportive Head Teacher, Terry Scott. The Reception team included the following people: Jacqui Granger, Kathryn Burgess, Lorna Griffin, Alison Sivyer, Ana Toledo, Leighann Pochetty, Liz Solomon, Rose Mullen, Vivien Redman, Donna Hoffland, Tracie Kettley and Fiona Mears. All had varying roles and made different contributions, leading to the successful year that the children experienced.

Obviously, the biggest thanks must go to the children for being children! And thanks also go to the parents for allowing me to use photos of their children in the book.

Preface to revised edition

The systems described in this book meet all the requirements of the revised EYFS, which came into effect in September 2012. Equally the ideas meet the requirements for an 'Outstanding' grade as described in the new OFSTED framework which came into effect in January 2012. Thus the purpose of writing this preface is to re-assure the reader with regard to both documents.

If we look first at the new OFSTED framework, the main difference for early years practitioners within schools is that there will no longer be a separate judgement for early years. There will be one judgement for the whole school. However, the reports that have been written since January do make separate comments about the early years provision. With regard to the child-led approach described in this book, it is clear that such an approach matches many of the descriptors for 'Outstanding' in the new framework.

For example within the 'Quality of Teaching', the outstanding descriptors include the following statements:

- Teachers plan astutely and set challenging tasks based on systematic, accurate assessment of pupils' prior skills, knowledge and understanding.
- Teachers and other adults generate high levels of enthusiasm for, participation in and commitment to learning.
- Teaching promotes pupils' high levels of resilience, confidence and independence when they tackle challenging activities.

The Reception Year In Action describes how planning is based on observations and assessments of each child in a spontaneous cycle. The book also goes into great detail about how the role of the adult is crucial in this cycle. The adults must be sensitive, responsive and flexible so that no learning opportunity is missed. With regard to the third point, the emphasis on the development of these personal and social skills runs through the whole book. It is the key to the success of a system which allows the children to pursue their own interests. This would not be possible without high levels of resilience, confidence and independence as they tackle the challenges that they set themselves.

Within the 'Behaviour and Safety' outstanding descriptors, there are some equally interesting statements:

- Pupils make an exceptional contribution to a safe, positive learning environment. They make every effort to ensure that others learn and thrive in an atmosphere of respect and dignity.
- Pupils show very high levels of engagement, courtesy, collaboration and cooperation in and out of lessons. They have excellent, enthusiastic attitudes to learning, enabling lessons to proceed without interruption.
- They are highly adept at managing their own behaviour in the classroom and in social situations.

In these statements it is clear that the emphasis on personal, social and emotional development is key and this is the message given throughout this book. In addition the phrase 'high levels of engagement' is very important. If children are pursuing their own interests – as this book is advocating – then their levels of engagement will be high. It is within this enthusiasm that the sensitive interaction from the adults can support and extend the learning possibilities.

One final comment with regard to OFSTED is that the emphasis is on 'progress, progress, progress'. Of course the data that shows progress over time will be studied. However, the inspectors will want to see progress within very short periods – sometimes as short as twenty minutes. Many practitioners are concerned about this. However, if you work in the spontaneous way described in this book, you are making assessments and plans in a moment-by-moment cycle. Therefore examples of progress will be occurring throughout the day. The adults are free to engage with the children in their interests and pursuits and the children will use the adults as a resource to help them with their learning. If an inspector observes a practitioner interacting with a child – answering a question, modelling a skill, providing vocabulary or giving suggestions, then they have observed progress in that child's development. This may need to be pointed out to the inspector, but the progress will be occurring – in almost every moment of every day.

I hope it is clear from these comments that in light of the new OFSTED framework, at De Bohun School, we will not be changing the way we work in our early years classes. We will be ready to enlighten the inspectors when they arrive and the children will be enthused and excited to demonstrate the progress they are making.

Similarly, the revised EYFS is not causing a revolution in our practice at De Bohun School. All the systems that we have in place, and which are described in this book, meet the requirements of the revised document. Again, I will quote a few pertinent sections and explain how they fit into a system of child-led learning with spontaneous planning.

There are two main changes within the document that will affect Reception classes: an increase in the number of areas of learning – from 6 areas to 7; and a reduction in the number of early learning goals from 69 to just 17. The extra area of learning has come about by splitting the Literacy element of CLLD from the language element. However, neither of these changes will have any effect on the organisation or provision for the children. The changes will occur in the planning and record-keeping documents. Thus the planning sheets (in Appendix C) have been amended to include the seven areas of learning. We have also amended our Foundation Stage Profile records to reflect the new Early Learning Goals. These changes will not affect the children or their experience of school in any way.

Within the rest of the revised document there are some statements which are very clear and very welcome and others which are far more ambiguous and open to interpretation. I will give some examples.

Paragraph 1.7 starts with the words 'Practitioners must consider the individual needs, interests, and stage of development of each child in their care, and must use this information to plan a challenging and enjoyable experience for each child in all areas of learning and development.' The children at De Bohun School are able to demonstrate their needs, interests and stage of development by pursuing their own interests in an enabling environment. The staff observe and support them so that they develop in all areas of learning. Thus the system described in the book will meet this requirement completely.

Paragraph 1.9 starts 'Each area of learning and development must be implemented through planned, purposeful play and through a mix of adult-led and child-initiated activity. Play is essential for children's development, building their confidence as they learn to explore, to think about problems, and relate to others. Children learn by leading their own play, and by taking part in play which is guided by adults. There is an ongoing judgement to be made by practitioners about the balance between activities led by children, and activities led or guided by adults. Practitioners must respond to each child's emerging needs and interests, guiding their development through warm, positive inter-action.' The system at De Bohun describes how children pursue their own interests and adults may join them and support them in their pursuits. This is then a mixture of 'child-led' and 'adult-guided' activity – even though the initial ideas are all from the children. Thus the requirements of the new document are being met.

The paragraph continues: 'As children grow older, and as their development allows, it is expected that the balance will gradually shift towards more activities led by adults, to help children prepare for more formal learning, ready for Year 1.' This is one of the state-ments that is ambiguous and open to interpretation. The word 'must' which appears so often in the revised document is not contained in this sentence. The crucial phrase is 'as their development allows'. Children in Reception classes are at a stage in their develop-ment when the best way for them to learn is through active, self-initiated activity. If they are making good progress, then that demonstrates that the provision is meeting their developmental needs. In terms of becoming more formal in preparation for Year 1, at De Bohun School, and in many schools now, the Year 1 classes are not very formal at the start of the year and therefore we do not need to prepare for this in Reception.

Paragraph 1.10 states 'In planning and guiding children's activities, practitioners must reflect on the different ways that children learn and reflect these in their practice. Three characteristics of effective teaching and learning are: playing and exploring . . . active learning . . . creating and thinking critically.' This is exactly the message given throughout this book! The diary sections in 'The Reception Year In Action' are full of examples of exactly this type of learning.

Children have a natural desire to explore, communicate, create and learn. This book describes a system to use in Early Years classes which allows this natural desire to be harnessed and celebrated – with wonderful results. Both the new OFSTED framework and the revised EYFS framework acknowledge the value of such a system and it contin-ues to bring joy to the children at De Bohun School.

June 2012

Introduction

Guiding principles

I have been teaching at De Bohun School for over 20 years and am striving to work in the best possible way for children in the Foundation Stage. During my career there have been numerous government initiatives, some of which I have embraced and others I have not. I constantly question new ideas and will resist their introduction if I think they are inappropriate. Thus, in 1999, during an OFSTED inspection, 70 per cent of my lessons were classed as 'failing' because the children were 'playing'. I was told by the inspector that 'The children have had their play in the nursery!' In contrast to this, our Foundation Stage was rated 'outstanding' in a recent OFSTED inspection when the inspector again saw the children 'playing'. When the Literacy Hour was introduced I was criticised because I did not adhere to the timing guidelines and was told that 'four-year-olds are perfectly capable of sitting on the carpet for 40 minutes!' Again I refused to follow these guidelines and a few years later there was a shift away from this pressure in Reception classes.

As practitioners we are in the best possible position to know what is appropriate for young children and what is not. We need to be more confident and assertive in the choices we make. The children in the Foundation Stage at De Bohun are happy, confident and enthusiastic about school. They have the foundations needed to become life-long learners. This book will explain how to achieve this. The ideas I present apply equally to preschools, nurseries and Reception classes. The principles apply to all children, whether from a deprived or a privileged background, whether they have special needs or not, whether they speak English or not, and whatever their style of learning.

The central principle in my practice is that the children follow their own interests. Children have a natural desire to explore, communicate, create and learn. Our job is to establish an environment (meaning the provision, the people and the atmosphere) where this is possible. One vital part of this is to ensure that each child feels safe, valued and important within the setting. Firm boundaries and expectations with regard to behaviour and relationships are established and enforced from day one. Staggered intake of small groups allows adults to concentrate on this vital aspect of our work. Self-discipline is also key, and both these topics are explained in further detail in Chapter 1. Once this enabling environment is established, the next job is to observe, support and extend the children in their pursuits.

This approach is daunting for many practitioners and parents. They are unsure about how the children will 'learn' if they are not 'taught' by the teachers. This book shows that the children do, in fact, thrive when a Reception class is organised and managed by the adults, but led by the children. They excel if they are in a stimulating environment that is carefully organised. They learn and develop when they are closely observed and the observations used to support their 'next steps'. They take risks and surpass expectations when they have clear routines and boundaries, combined with a supportive staff and an enabling environment. They see learning as an integral part of their lives when information and links are made between school and home. This book gives teachers the practical ideas they need in order to work with confidence in this way. It gives parents an insight into the magical world that is a Reception class where the children lead the learning.

Structure of the book

The book attempts to describe all aspects of a complete year in a Reception class – a huge undertaking. The organisation of the book aims to present the information in a meaningful structure. There are 11 chapters in the book – one for each month of the school year. Each chapter is divided into three sections – 'Organisation', 'Environment' and 'Diary'.

The 'Organisation' sections deal with various aspects of Early Years teaching, such as risk assessment and planning. They cover topics relevant to the particular month but also ongoing issues and subjects for debate. The 'Environment' sections describe various areas of the environment – both indoors and outdoors. These are spread throughout the book and are not linked to particular months. The 'Diary' sections are records of real events from that month – highlighting development and learning.

De Bohun School: background information

De Bohun School is situated in the London Borough of Enfield and has some of the highest rates of mobility, special needs, English as an Additional Language and free school meals in the country.

In recent years there have been increasing numbers of Reception-age children in our borough and we have had to take extra children. In September 2009, we had 43 children in the Reception year group. Rather than put these children into two small classes, we opted to have one large classroom with access to the garden. We employed an NQT, Jacqui, and extra Early Years classroom assistants. This meant that we had two teachers (myself and Jacqui) and two support staff in the class at all times. With students and special needs support staff, there were often around 50 people in the Reception unit. Every adult in the team worked to ensure that the children had a wonderful year.

Although there are two children with extreme additional needs in the class, I will not be describing their year in detail as it is outside the remit of this book. However, I would say that both children have made huge progress during the year, without the need for withdrawal from the main class. They have been allowed to follow their own interests and with firm, consistent boundaries they have adhered to the same routines and expectations as all the other children.

Theory and practice

Many people have influenced the way I work, not least my father. He was educated in the early 1930s by Nora Black (a contemporary of Susan Isaacs). He went to her 'experimental' boarding school where very young children were encouraged to pursue their own interests and given an amazing amount of freedom. My father became a cabinetmaker and spent his free time working for the Woodcraft Folk, a children's organisation striving for social change. Our family holidays were spent camping with the Woodcraft Folk and then more camping in France. The link to my current teaching is clear: outdoor provision and woodwork are key features in my work. When I read the work of Susan Isaacs, it sounds exactly like my father and closely matches my approach to education. I have always believed that 'nurture' combines with 'nature' to influence individual children. My experiences as a parent, a teacher and a foster carer have confirmed this 'interactionist' stance. Our work at De Bohun is an example of the theory in practice.

Where to now?

In attempting to write down how our class is run, I have realised that working as an Early Years practitioner is a very complex job. In addition, every setting is unique, with different assets as well as various problems, and its own distinct group of families. There is no single answer, no one right way to do things. However, we are responsible for these children at a very important and impressionable stage in their lives, a stage that they only get to live through once. It is our job to make their experience as beneficial as possible. I am constantly questioning my practice and wondering what could be changed and improved. Twenty years ago we had no outdoor provision in our school. Now we are recognised as having some of the best provision, and yet still we strive for more. For everyone in Early Years, we need to reflect on our current practice and try new ways of working.

1 September

This chapter is structured differently to the others to reflect the unique nature of this month. The Organisation section is divided into two parts, with the Environment section in between. This is to emphasise how vital it is to do preparation work – both in terms of getting to know the families **and** setting up the environment – **before** the children start school. The unique timetable for September is explained and, in terms of setting up the class and garden, the general principles are described. I also explain home visits, our induction programme and how our daily routine is organised. In the Diary section, I describe the earliest work to start the development of self-discipline and look briefly at the introduction of woodwork.

SEPTEMBER: TO DO LIST

- Settle Year 1 children into their new class.
- Arrange classroom and garden.
- Label resources – with words and pictures.
- Select children to form groups for staggered intake.
- Carry out home visits.
- Amend/add to resources according to information gathered.
- Collect information from previous settings.
- Pass on information to school office.
- Flag up Special Needs issues with the SENCO.
- Set up a folder for each child.
- Induct new staff into planning/record-keeping systems.
- Stagger intake over two weeks.
- Concentrate on establishing ground rules and routines.
- Reassess and evaluate class and garden organisation.
- Complete and collate entry assessments.

September timetable

September is a unique month for anyone working in Early Years; a period when preparation is carried out that will have lasting effects. At De Bohun, we delay our start date by two or three days (as shown by the yellow highlights below) so the whole team can work to implement changes and set up the class and garden in the best possible way. Many head teachers need convincing of the value gained by this. It is vital to explain in detail what the time will be used for and how it will affect the whole year. If your setting does not run on a school year, I would still argue for these 'closure days' at some point in the year.

Week 1	2 whole school INSET days
	1 day supporting in Year 1 (team teaching to ensure the children settle happily into the new year group.)
	==2 days carrying out large-scale tasks in the class and garden==
Week 2	Home visits
Week 3	2 days home visits
	==1 day making final preparations in the class and garden==
	2 days – first groups attend (half-day sessions)
Week 4	Remaining groups attend for half-day sessions

Figure 1.1 September timetable

Thus, by the end of September, the class and garden are set up and all the children are attending for half-day sessions.

The work that is done in the class and garden during this period will depend on the individual situation of the setting. Organisation is key – decide on priorities, allocate tasks and celebrate the results. There may be no budget at all, but that should not prevent change. For example, it costs nothing to dig over an area of hard ground to make a digging pit, to clear out and de-clutter the storage areas, to design and discuss a new planning sheet, to set up a folder for each child or to reorganise the creative area indoors. As you read this book you will come across ideas that will require thought, adaptation to your setting and time to put them into practice. I have an ongoing wish list for my class, and as soon as I get to the end of the list, there is another list below. You may find it necessary to make different lists: one for long-term vision (e.g. including some aspects of building work or staffing), a second for ideas that have a financial cost (prioritised once any budget is known) and a third for ideas that just require time. The two or three preparation days in September can give your team a chance to make some of these changes. Involvement of all staff ensures a sense of ownership of any changes and responsibility for their maintenance during the year. New areas or ideas then have the best possible chance of success.

Setting up the environment

General principles

At De Bohun, we strive to ensure that the **children feel safe and confident so that they can explore and play independently.**

Ground rules are few, but are established from day 1 to ensure that every child feels able to explore freely. We are all **respectful towards each other.** This is taught by example and intervention whenever disrespect or unkindness is observed. Everyone must **walk and talk indoors** – if anyone wants to run and shout, they are directed to the garden. Everyone needs to **take care of the class and garden** and the things in it. During the first few weeks at school, the establishment of these expectations takes the majority of our time. We invest this time at the start of the year and see long-lasting benefits very quickly.

We **constantly review the provision and layout** of the class and garden. For example, if we observe that the carpet area is constantly overcrowded, we will try to make this area larger. The layout keeps certain activities away from others – e.g. quiet/noisy (such as book corner and role play area), wet/dry (such as water and computers) or messy/clean (such as painting and small world play).

Self-service units allow children to be independent.

We do not set resources out – **the children select the resources and activities themselves** (see Daily Routines below). The children should not need to approach an adult to ask for glue or to ask to go to the toilet. The **interactions with adults should be far more meaningful and valuable** (see Chapter 5). A good way to assess your own environment is to think about or monitor the reasons why children approach the adults. If it is to sort out disputes, then this is an area that needs focus. If it is to request resources, then this needs attention. If it is to ask permission to do something, then maybe the boundaries and agreements need restating. As new issues arise we adapt the provision or spend time working on a particular aspect of behaviour.

We have removed everything from the class and garden that is not for the children to access on a daily basis. Thus all adults' belongings, special resources and resource boxes have been moved out of the classroom and stored elsewhere. Whenever possible, we replace inappropriate storage with units that allow the children to 'self-serve' resources. We are always on the lookout for furniture

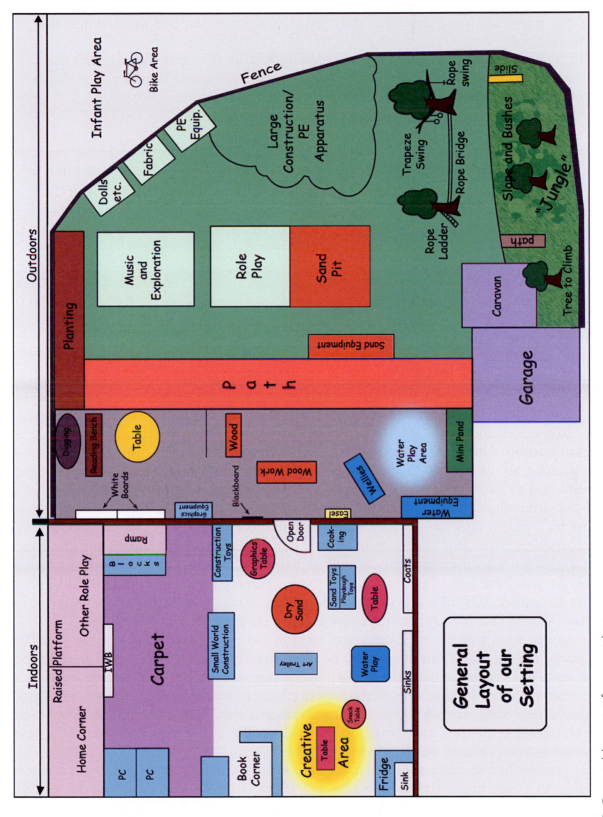

Figure 1.2 General layout of our setting

being discarded by other classes – often for use outdoors – a coating of gloss paint or a tarpaulin cover can mean the furniture gets a new lease of life. **Storage units are labelled with photos and words** to show what they should contain. In this way, the children can be independent when tidying up as well. Because the children get the resources out themselves, they also know where to put them when they have finished.

In the following chapters, the detailed provision in each area is described. However, the principle is constant – careful organisation and labelling that allows independent access to a wide variety of high-quality resources.

Many settings share an outdoor space between two or three classes. It is often a good idea to share indoor spaces too. For example, if you have two interconnecting classrooms, then have single provision over the two rooms. You can then have one large, but well resourced, role play area, one large creative area, and so on, rather than small areas in each room. The classes can still split for carpet sessions to keep these manageable and effective.

Home visits

We home-visit every child that joins our Reception class. It is a chance to start building a relationship with each family. It is vital that all adults involved with the child (at school and at home) feel part of a team that is working for the best interests of the child. At the home visit the family can talk in detail about their child, including any concerns and expectations. They can also explain the family background and culture. The 'school' has a chance to gather all this information from the family, to answer queries and concerns and to explain how the Reception class is organised (stressing the benefits of a child-led curriculum). Each visit lasts about 40 minutes and two adults go together – one to chat to a parent and one to play with the child. We take a selection of toys, books, paper, pencils, scissors and photos from school. Hopefully, these will engage the child and allow a glimpse into their interests as well as helping them to look forward to starting school. We also have lots of information to pass to parents, forms to complete and information to gather. We take school sweatshirts and book bags with us for parents to purchase. We fill in a form/checklist as we chat, to ensure nothing gets missed.

We do not send out the start dates and sessions before we have met the families. We have start dates in mind but these may be altered according to issues that arise at the home visit. For example, we usually start the youngest children first. However, if at a home visit we discover that one of the oldest children is very timid, then we may give them an earlier start date. We stress to all parents that they will need to stay with their child at school until they are settled and confident. For some, this will only be a few minutes; for others it may be six weeks.

This year we had several issues raised at home visits. One mother reported that her son is unable to clean himself after going to the toilet if he doesn't have wet wipes. We suggested that she spend time in the following couple of weeks helping her son overcome this. Two mums said they were starting work so needed their children in full-time school as soon as possible. They also said they would be using breakfast club and after-school club. We stressed that we would do our best to settle the children as quickly as

Name of child: Address: First language: Religion: Ethnicity: DOB: Tel:	Parent/Guardians name(s): In case of an emergency contact: Tel:
	Who can collect? Tel:

Tell us about your child – preschool experience, previous transitions, self-help skills, interests, family members, concerns (keep us informed of any changes).

Waiting list for other schools:
Temporary housing:

Allergies/medical history:	Food – diet – school dinners – cost and free school dinners – eligibility and form.	
Child-led curriculum Routines – sessions **8.50–11.30 12.40–3.15** Uniform, clothing, shoes, coat – name everything (jumper and book bag) Start date and time:	Take individual photo of child Request/collect/take a family photo	Sign permission slips (trips/photos) Breakfast club 8 am FREE After school club – 5.15pm £3

Figure 1.3 Home visit checklist

possible but that the interests of the child had to be paramount. We urged these parents to try to get a support network in place in case their child did not settle as quickly as they hoped. I was reminded of something I heard when visiting settings in Australia. A practitioner said, 'We are not child-storage facilities'. This made me smile, but there is a serious message here. Schools in the UK are now expected to try to offer extended hours to allow parents to work if they wish. However, who benefits from this? Are we becoming 'child-storage facilities'? What are the long-term effects on children who are in childcare from 8 am to 6 pm from the age of four months? When parents are pressurising us to take their children into school full-time, we need to be sure that it is the best thing for the child.

Family photos

When we send the home visit appointment, we request a family photo be available for us to take to school to be displayed in class. (We provide the frames.) If the family do not have a photo, we offer to take one with the school camera. They look great and are a lovely focal point when children first come to school. These can be seen in Chapter 3.

Induction

At De Bohun, we have developed an induction programme resulting in the children settling quickly and, within a week, many are ready to stay full-time. We put the children into groups according to age and start the youngest 16 children first (eight in the morning, eight in the afternoon). This gives them two days in the class before the next group of older children arrive. We have groups in the morning and the afternoon. This keeps the numbers low during the induction period but allows all children to start school in a short period. It also ensures that adults are able to work closely with each child in their first few days to establish the vital ground rules and expectations. Parents stay with their child until the child is happy for them to leave. The parents are a huge asset during this settling period. We show them how the children need to self-register and they then teach this to their child. We encourage the parents to show the children around the setting, including the toilets. We ask them to explain to their child that they can play indoors or outside and can get out anything they wish to use, and they also encourage them to tidy up when they want to do something else.

In these first few days and weeks, we introduce **Makaton** signing for numerous basic words and this continues throughout the year. It is valuable for all children, helping them to communicate if they find this difficult – e.g. if they are shy, do not speak English or have a language delay.

This year, all the children who had attended our nursery settled without any problems. It seems our transition work has done its job for them. Also, the vast majority of children who have been on our list since last term are fine too – they have attended play sessions and I have visited them at their preschool setting as well as at home.

Only two children are finding it difficult to adjust. These are both boys who have been in all-day childcare since age 4 months. Both are tearful and reluctant for their parent to leave. When a child has been in one setting virtually since birth and then transfers to a school setting, the transition is bound to be difficult. They are leaving everything that is familiar. The mothers in both cases were very distressed and insisted, 'But they are used to leaving me'. We discussed this and pointed out that it was the complete change of setting and staff that was the issue, rather than leaving the parent.

Both mothers agreed to stay, and gradually, over a period of three weeks, the boys settled.

All the children attend for half-days until parents *and* staff feel they are ready to cope with a full day. We have drawn up a list of criteria that we feel a child should meet in order to be at school full-time. This is explained at the home visit and referred to if parents ask about full-time attendance.

The child should be able to:

a) Separate from carer easily.
b) Move independently around the playground and class (both indoor and outdoor areas).
c) Stay awake and energetic throughout the session.
d) Be happy in the large playground.
e) Cope with changes of adults in the classroom without distress.
f) Stay within set boundaries of the playground and class (both indoor and outdoor areas).
g) Behave appropriately (and non-aggressively) for the majority of time.
h) Manage their own personal hygiene.

Figure 1.4 Criteria to be met for full-time attendance in Reception

The majority meet the criteria during their first week and nearly all do so over a period of about three weeks, and then attend full-time.

Daily routines

We organise the day to **maximise the periods of sustained uninterrupted play** to encourage in-depth exploration. Some head teachers will need convincing that four-year-olds should not be in assembly and do not need to have PE lessons or ICT lessons etc. *outside* the Reception area. Our children are free to follow their own interests for long uninterrupted periods. They are not disturbed in their play to 'go to PE', 'go out to play' or 'do some work with the teacher'. The morning and afternoon sessions are equal length. This is particularly important at the start of the autumn term when half the class attend in the morning and half in the afternoon.

The question of direct whole-class or group teaching in the classroom is an even bigger area of contention and debate. At De Bohun, we have seen that **as the amount of direct whole-class and group teaching has reduced, the attainment in all areas, by all children, has increased.** We are fortunate to have a head teacher who was willing to take a leap of faith and allow the staff to be led by the children.

The Reception children have their lunch at 11.30 am, which means that they have the hall to themselves for 30 minutes, avoiding the stress of a noisy dining hall. After lunch they go into the infant playground and have this to themselves for 20 minutes before Year 1 joins them.

In many settings, lunchtime is organised so that the Reception children go back into their own garden for the lunch break. They are either supervised by mealtime supervisors or by one or two of the Reception staff. I have not found anyone who is completely happy with this arrangement. The children necessarily play differently because they are restricted to being outdoors with fewer staff. Resources are damaged and children become upset through increased conflicts occurring as a result of being in a crowded space with fewer resources. As stated, at De Bohun we have the lunch 'playtime' in the infant playground, and this is not ideal either. However, at least the Reception garden is not damaged and the children have a large space in which to run around. This is an ongoing area of discussion and review.

The daily routine is shown below. **The door to the garden is open from the moment the children arrive.** The children come into the class, self-register by moving one of their name labels from their peg to a numbered board and then select something to do – either indoors or outdoors. Quite often, they move around, chatting to other children and to adults before settling to an activity. Note the highlighted sessions are over two hours long.

8.50 – 11.00 am	Children arrive at school and play in the Reception classroom and garden. (Wheeled toys are available between 9 am and 10 am in infant playground.)
11.00 – 11.15 am	Children tidy class and garden.
11.15 – 11.30 am	Children gather on carpet for large-group activity.
11.30 am	Parents collect children who are attending for morning session only.
11.30 – 12.00 noon	Lunch in hall with teacher.
12 noon – 12.20 pm	Reception children play in infant playground.
12.20 – 12.40 pm	Reception children play with Year 1 children in the infant playground.
12.40 – 2.50 pm	Afternnoon children arrive at school and join rest of class to play in the Reception classroom and garden.
2.50 – 3.05 pm	Children tidy class and garden.
3.05 – 3.20 pm	Children gather on carpet for large-group activity.

Figure 1.5 Daily routine

Diary extracts: examples of development and learning

In this section, I will explain the work we do to begin the development of self-discipline and also the early introduction of woodwork.

Ground rules

The children are only in school for one or two weeks during September. The time is spent establishing the ground rules and expectations (as explained above). Many visitors have asked me, 'But don't you start teaching them straight away?' My response is that we *are* teaching them from the moment they walk through the door – teaching them how they will be valued and cared for and what our expectations are. If this 'teaching' is successful, we will have a group of happy, relaxed children who can explore and learn independently. They play purposefully in all areas and look after each other, the class and the garden. The adults are then free to engage in valuable interactions of their choice, in areas where they can make a difference.

Conflict resolution

One vital part of this 'teaching' is that of **conflict resolution**. Each time a child comes to an adult to 'tell a tale', or each time an adult observes a conflict taking place, it is viewed as a teaching opportunity. The adult encourages the children to describe what has happened and then to say how they feel about this. The children are encouraged to talk to each other and to say things such as 'Don't do that, I don't like it!' or 'You have been on that rope for a long time. You need to get off now and let me have a turn' or 'Can I have that toy in a little while please?' It is the children who ultimately resolve the situation with their own words. Of course, they are also told that if the other child does not listen, then they should seek help from an adult. Children do respond differently when an adult is listening, but gradually they realise that they can resolve disputes themselves. They are praised for doing so and eventually it becomes automatic. This is one area that is commented on by every visitor to our setting. For example, the OFSTED inspector watched the class for 40 minutes and then said, 'They just get on, don't they?'

Woodwork introduction

While the numbers are still small we have allowed access to the woodwork bench so that we can teach the children the very simple rules – 'Only two children at a time' and 'Two hands on the saw'. This has worked very well and nearly all the children have opted to have a turn and been shown how to put the wood in the vice for sawing.

The stock of wood can be seen on the shelving near the work bench.

They are also learning how to hammer a nail without hitting their fingers! Some lovely models have already been produced.

The children often make wooden models and use other materials to complete their work.

By the end of September all the children were attending part-time, displaying confidence and enjoyment in their new environment. The foundations had been laid for a successful year ahead.

2 October

In October the majority of the class will stay at school full-time and the children mix with a larger group each week. It is important that the class is well organised and everyone is clear about their role. Thus in this chapter we look in detail at our weekly routines, including the system of 'focus children', 'spontaneous planning', how we organise observations and how records are kept for each child. These systems are key to our success and are explained in detail. In the section describing the environment, I will look at reading and books in general, the art area indoors and the sand play area outside. The diary gives some wonderful examples of activities from this busy month, including several that were inspired by photos the children had taken at home and also trips outside the school boundaries.

OCTOBER: TO DO LIST

- Start first cycle of focus groups.
- Start first cycle of parent meetings.
- Continue to establish expectations and ground rules.
- Review and amend layout and provision.
- Assess each child against the full-time criteria and invite the majority to stay full-time.
- Update individual folders.

The weekly routine – including observations and planning

Focus children and parental involvement

On Friday each week we select the focus children for the following week. This is 10 per cent of the class – usually three children. Each child must be a focus child once each term. We have 43 children on roll and so choose four children. At the beginning of the year we tend to choose children who are already confident and settled, as a child who is still apprehensive may not like too much adult attention. As the year progresses, the choice of focus children is made on a weekly basis, either according to who appears to be making sudden progress or who we feel would benefit from the extra attention to move their development along. At the end of Friday we give each of the focus children a digital camera and an A4 consultation sheet for their parents to complete (see below). We speak to the parents concerned to explain the routine.

The children return the sheet and camera on the following Monday. During one of the 'carpet sessions', the photos from home are shown on the interactive whiteboard and a selection is printed to add to the child's folder (see below for details of folders). The children are encouraged to describe the photos, giving details of the people and events shown. The links to home are wonderful and the children see how experiences from

Next week we will be focusing on _____. We will be observing them while they play to find out more about their interests and how they are progressing. Please take some pictures of your child/family enjoying activities out of school.

We value the knowledge and understanding you have of your child and would really appreciate it if you would share this with us so that together we can plan activities to meet your child's needs. This will help us plan for their future learning and development.

Is there anything significant happening in your child's life at the moment, e.g. visits, holidays, new pets, family celebrations? Is there anything you would like to tell us about your child?

Do you have anything you would like to ask us about your child's progress and development in Reception?

Please return this sheet with the school camera by _____
so that we can add your thoughts and ideas to the planning process.

Please ensure that the camera is used with adult supervision, kept away from water and that no objects are placed on the camera's LED screen.

Figure 2.1 Planning for your child's learning journey

home are valued by the school; for example, we now have photos of families attending a mosque, children playing musical instruments, extended family members, etc.

Spontaneous planning for the focus children

I believe that we should not plan ahead for very young children. Their interests are 'in the moment' and need to be responded to immediately to gain the full value of the child's curiosity and engagement at that time. We have developed our 'planning' sheets so that they are a record of the activities that have happened. We refer to these 'planning sheets' as 'learning journeys' to reflect their content. The idea has been introduced in many Reception, nursery and preschool settings in the borough. Everyone agrees that, for the first time, they have a 'planning' format that is a true reflection of the events in the class.

On Monday morning we put up an A3 'learning journey' sheet for each of the focus children (see an example of a completed sheet on the next page). The sheet is blank apart from the name, date and a few notes in the top left-hand box. These notes are compiled after consultations with other staff members and from the sheet completed by the parents. Once the children arrive at school, the focus children become just that – a 'focus' for extra observation, attention and support. The children may be unaware that they are part of the focus group. We do not follow these children all day every day for the whole week – they would be totally overwhelmed. However, we do observe the children carefully and look for opportunities to discuss, extend or elaborate their activity. The following chapters give numerous examples of this.

Any adult who works in the class with a focus child adds to the learning journey sheet and so it becomes a record of the week. The box in the top right-hand corner is a way of checking that all areas of the curriculum have been covered, that the child has been observed indoors and out and that an adult has had conversations with the parents and the child during the week. It is rare to find a box without a tick. Some of the entries may simply be a record of an activity that the child has completed independently. However, it is important that most entries **include the adult interventions and outcomes**. This is a record of how the child has been supported in taking the 'next steps' in their journey. By the end of the week the sheets are full of notes and photos.

We make colour photocopies of these sheets – one to go in the child's folder and one for the teacher's file. By the end of the year, a teacher will have 90 sheets as a record of the year. Settings using this 'planning' system have, of course, adapted the sheet to suit their needs. The symbol 'T' indicates 'adult'.

By the end of the week we have got to know and understand the focus children in a way that we never could have hoped for in a more traditional way of teaching. By following their interests and talking to them for long periods, we gain an insight into their style of learning, abilities and knowledge. The learning journeys provide a wealth of information and have replaced isolated narrative observations and forward planning. The only time we would use a narrative observation is when we are concerned about a specific aspect of a child's behaviour and want to observe this in action.

In the week following their focus week, we invite the parents of the child into school for a discussion about the week and all that we have learnt about the child. We discuss any points that the parents have written on the consultation form and encourage them to add comments to the child's folder. Together we agree on possible areas for focus in future and how we can all help the child with these.

Each child is a focus child once per term, three times per year, and thus the parents have this opportunity to contribute and consult with us in this structured way each term. Of course they are able to chat to us at the start or end of each day as well.

Learning Journey For D   **Date** 7.6.10   **Week** 7

Identified Areas For Focus:
General: Continue to build Confidence in English
From Parents: Is she quiet at school? ✓
From Profile: One more-oneless than 5 objects. Rhyme. ✓

D saw new puppets + wanted to play with them. (T) suggested do a show with her friends. D said "You sit here and watch. How you do his?" (T) showed her how to put puppet on her hand. She started today with puppet.

Child made nos 1 & 2 for chairs in puppet theatre. (T) asked D what number was next. D said "3" than drew a 3, cut it out & attached it to chair.

Areas of Learning	Observations
PSED	✓
CLL	✓
PSRN	✓
KUW	✓
PD	✓
CD	✓
Obs indoors	✓
Obs outdoors	✓
Conversations with child	✓
Conversations with parent	
Parent meeting	✓

D put sand in plates, bowls, cups and tea pots. (T) observed D talking to her friends 'We need more cakes, if we dont have more we cant have the party.' D then counted all the cakes 1:1 up to 16. She then start naming children in the class to the cakes (T) suggested she makes a real cake tomorrow.
Next step: cake design and ingredients list.

D wanted o look for frogs in the pd, when at the pond saw a dead hedgehog floating 'Oh no it dead.' D asked how she thought it had died 'it can't swim.' We need to get it and bury it. (T) asked how can we get it out? (T) got

The hedgehog out of the pond. D said 'it smell.' we need to dig a hole quick.' D and a group of children dug a hole (T) encouraged group to think about the size of the hole and will the hedgehog fit. D went on to make a cross using two bits of wood 'It go heaven now.'

D drew a picture of princess, she then covered her picture in elastic bands. 'I'm making a guitar picture.' She used a nail to hammer a tiny piece & bond to the wood. She asked for help after

C wrote ingredients list for cake, she used her knowledge of initial sounds o most letters were correctly formed.

D was encouraged t read the cooking instructions. (T) encouraged D to use the picture cues - by page 2 she was confident to read them to the group. Ramuna asked if she had balanced the butter, D told her 'No it has to go down.' Another child said it dont matter. D said 'it doesnt matter. When mixing the cake D said 'it looks like banana because its yellow.

General: Confidence when speaking English. Sentence structure.
From Parents: Making friends. writing.
From Profile: Addition + Subtraction.

Figure 2.2 Individual learning journey

Spontaneous planning for the rest of the class

'What about the rest of the class?' This is a question I am asked over and over. The answer is simple. The other children carry on with their own learning journeys (even though they are not recorded in this way). Sometimes they journey on their own, sometimes with a friend or a group and sometimes by joining an activity with one of the focus children. Also, as explained above, the adults are not totally absorbed with the focus children. They are often free to support other individuals or groups. We use a separate A3 sheet to record such activities. Again, this is started on a Monday and completed during the week. This sheet is kept in the teacher's file and a copy is put out on the parents' noticeboard for them to look at. A completed example is shown on the next page.

Observations of individuals, including individual folders

All adults working in the class make observations about the children. We are keen to record 'Wow!' moments – when a child does or says something that demonstrates progress or skill in a particular area. This would include a record of the adult intervention if relevant. If appropriate, a photo is taken to accompany the observation. These notes are written on sticky labels and dropped into a wallet in a box file.

Each child has a wallet in the box file and these quickly fill up with observations, photos and pieces of work. Periodically (at least once every half-term and usually once every four weeks), these wallets are emptied and everything is transferred to the children's individual folders. Ideally, this would be done with the children at school, and sometimes this is possible. The children certainly enjoy sticking in their photos and describing them to an adult. However, it is very time-consuming and is often done during PPA time or at weekends. All adults contribute to these folders, but it is ultimately the teacher's responsibility to update them. In some settings key workers are responsible for the folders of their key children.

The **individual folders** are A4 ring binders and there is one for each child. They are kept in a low unit where the children can access them whenever they wish. There is often a group looking at their folders together. Whenever possible, I join the group and scribe some of their comments in the folder. We do this with a green pen and date the entry to distinguish it from normal observations etc. This is a simple way of bringing the child's voice into their folder. For example, Jenna said, 'Look, I cut out that heart and put glitter on it'.

Everything relating to a particular child is kept in their folder (with the exception of confidential information) – reports from previous settings, observations, pieces of work, photos, learning journey sheets, consultation sheets, assessments etc. These folders include the Foundation Stage Profile. The folders are a wonderful record of the year, and at the end of the summer term they are shown to and discussed with the Year 1 teachers. If a child needs to continue with a Foundation Stage curriculum in Year 1, the folder continues to be used. Eventually, all the children take them home and they become a treasured keepsake.

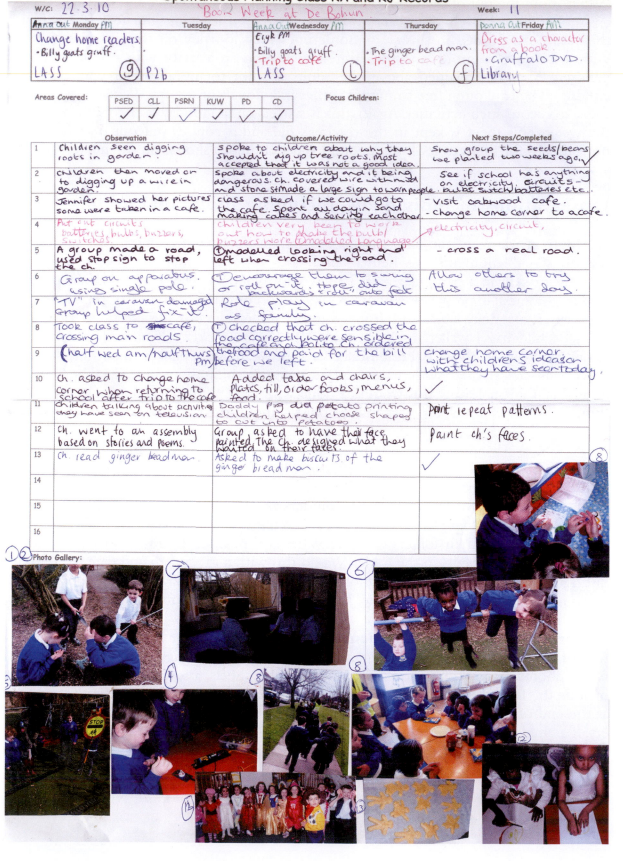

Figure 2.3 Record of activities in the class

The children can look at their folders whenever they wish.

Setting up the environment

Books and reading

Jacqui has set up a cosy book corner in the classroom and books are available in other areas of the class and garden too: information books in the creative area; books to 'read' to babies in the home corner; magazines in the 'waiting room' at the doctors; books with CDs in the listening area; books on gardening near the digging area; information books about minibeasts in the garden; books about cars, motorbikes, bridges and buildings near the large construction area; a variety of books in the caravan; and cookery books in the cooking area. They are an integral part of the setting.

A cosy book corner.

The provision is constantly reviewed and new books provided as required. When new topics arise, groups are taken to the school library to get information books. The children quickly realise that books provide information as well as entertainment.

In the book corner we have cushions and a small bench, a CD player with headphones and books on CD. There is a canopy above to create a cosy atmosphere and the individual folders are kept in this area too. There are also story sacks with books and props for children to act out favourite stories. In the garden we also have a reading bench, which is just a garden bench covered with bright fabric and cushions. A box containing a selection of books is placed next to the bench. Because adults are available to respond to the requests of children, there are often small groups listening to stories that they have chosen.

Adults read to children indoors and outside.

It is worth considering carefully the position of your book corner. In classes where this is a shared space (used also for, e.g. block play), it is rare to see children reading in that area. However, if its status is raised, valued and separated from other resources, it suddenly becomes far more attractive and more likely to be used effectively.

Children want to learn to read. However, if forced to 'read' they can easily be put off. Reading is an integral part of the environment we have created. When children are trying to read something, that is the perfect opportunity to engage with them and support them. The table below lists some reasons or situations in which young children would want to read and also lists some strategies we use to support this.

Reasons to read and strategies to support reading

Children want/need to read in order to . . .	make a cake make something seen in a book hear a favourite story share their own writing get information/answer questions access computer games choose food from a menu read a letter/card they receive find resources
The support, tools, strategies that are given/taught by adults include . . .	picture cues reading to children modelling reading skills e.g. tracking left to right labelling resources making books on CD available scribing for children and reading back their work supporting children with phonics and structured phonic work teaching sight vocabulary (tricky words) using a reading scheme when appropriate

Figure 2.4 Reading

Creative 'art' area indoors

The indoor art area is always popular. All resources are stored in labelled units that are accessible to the children.

Independent art work.

The resources available include:

- art and craft books for reference
- paint (numerous types and colours)
- implements (brushes of different sizes, rubber implements, cotton buds, sponges, printing blocks, straws etc.)
- paper and card (varying in size, colour and thickness)
- tissue paper and shiny paper
- sticky paper sheets and shapes
- fabric (various types, sizes and colours)
- sewing materials (including threaded needles, binka and thread)
- string, wool and ribbon
- glue (various types)
- pens, felt tips, crayons and pencils (large variety)
- scissors (varying styles and cutting patterns)
- recycled greetings cards
- recycled boxes, tubes and tubs (on labelled shelving unit)
- Sellotape, masking tape and coloured insulating tape
- staplers
- hole punch
- old magazines and catalogues to cut up
- collage materials (large variety – e.g. pasta, sequins, stars, bottle tops, fabric pieces, coloured paper etc.)
- natural materials collected from the garden (leaves, twigs etc.)
- clay
- clipboards
- aprons
- drying rack
- storage area for ongoing/completed 3D work
- rubbish bin.

Such wonderful resources inspire the most reluctant child to become involved. Since the children select the resources and organise the activity, we never have a display of, e.g. 30 daffodils or 30 gingerbread men. It is not important for every child to do every activity. The children participate in activities that are important and meaningful to them. In this way, their co-operation and enthusiasm is a given – there is no need to persuade or coax them to be involved. The reduction in stress for children and staff is considerable.

The art area requires daily restocking and tidying. It must remain organised and inviting to ensure that it is used in a purposeful way. Many children spend time making things that they have no interest in later on or the next day. This is fine – the time has not been 'wasted' (as some adults fear) – the process was important and absorbing for the child; the final product is not so valuable. Other children will ask for something they made a month ago! We sort through the finished pieces on a daily basis and gradually learn which we need to keep, display or discard.

Sand play outdoors

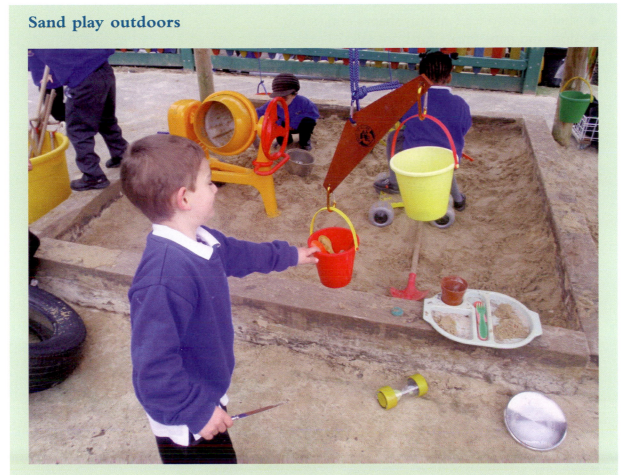

Children love to be *in* the sand.

This area is one of the most popular outdoors. We have a large sand pit made from four railway sleepers (each measuring 8 feet). These can be purchased ready-treated, and need simply to be placed on hard ground, filled with washed silver sand, and covered with a tarpaulin at night. We have a shelter over the sand pit, which is wooden and to which we attach pulleys and buckets. We have a table, chairs, a cupboard and a cooker beside the sand pit to accommodate the 'cooking' that inevitably takes place. The children transport water to the sand pit too. Resources from other areas are combined with the sand if necessary and if appropriate. For example, it is acceptable to get paper and pens to make flags or to bring plastic dinosaurs to live in the cave, but it is not acceptable to use all cars in the sand as their wheels get clogged up and damaged. Children are involved in these decisions so that the logic is clear and future choices will be more careful. We have T-shirts hanging up beside the sand pit for children to put over their white T-shirts. This is to avoid sand stains that make parents angry!

All resources are stored nearby in accessible labelled units and include:

● buckets (various sizes and shapes)
● spades, rakes and trowels
● brooms
● wheelbarrows
● sand moulds
● vehicles (cars and trucks of various sizes)

- shells and stones (various shapes and sizes)
- pots and pans (from car boot sales)
- cake tins (various shapes and sizes)
- mixing bowls
- jugs, bottles and teapots
- wooden spoons, ladles, whisks etc.
- sieves
- cups, saucers, plates and cutlery
- buckets attached to pulleys
- balance attached to rope
- toy cement-mixer.

Do not aim for a tidy sand area outdoors – the children will be missing out on so much if you do. The combination of sand and water is fascinating to young children and their experiments do make a mess. As long as the area is returned to some order at the end of the session, then it is fine.

Several of these children are wearing the blue T-shirts to protect their clothes.

The levels of involvement displayed are often higher here than anywhere else. It is a vital resource and should be a priority for any setting.

Diary extracts: examples of development and learning

In this section, there are examples of activities from many areas as well as activities outside the boundaries of the garden and even the school. Experiences that take the children out of the school environment often act as a catalyst for extended learning in many areas. Other extracts show how the photos taken at home by the focus children stimulate activities at school.

A visit to the pet shop

The first week of October was fantastic. Jacqui had got agreement from the head teacher for us to have two guinea pigs in school. She had purchased the cage and a run. We decided to take advantage of the low numbers and take the children to the pet shop to make the purchase. We hired two minibuses for the day and took the morning group and then the afternoon group to the pet shop to buy these.

Two boys in particular, who had not settled very well, came alive in the shop, and on return to school they participated in settling the animals and then moving to play in other areas of the class and garden.

Animals can have a huge impact in an Early Years setting, motivating even the most timid children to become involved.

On returning from the shop, we realised we had not bought a bowl for the food. One boy said, 'Let's make one'. The clay is always available and so several children set to and made pinch pots to hold the food. A few days later the pots had been fired. They were then painted and taken up to the hutch.

Without a pre-written plan for the day or week it is possible to respond to events immediately. It was a true oversight on our part not to have bought food pots for the guinea pigs and a genuine solution was found by the children. The adults were available to teach children how to make pinch pots and discuss clay, its properties and the need for it to be fired etc.

Several children thought the hutch needed a label and so two boys (who we had never seen put anything on paper) sat down, wrote the name (Max) and drew a picture. We discussed what would happen to the signs if they were left out in the rain and so decided they needed laminating. The boys went and watched this being done. When the guinea pigs were in the run, it was obvious to the children that they were trying to hide but had no shelter. Five children ran inside and found a big box, which they insisted on painting before taking back outside for a shelter for the run.

Photos from home lead to activities at school

Cake making

Isabel, one of the focus children this week, had photos of herself baking cakes at home and said she would like to do this at school. We asked her to write a shopping list. She drew a flower for the flour, an egg. and did an 's' for sugar! She also wrote a few other letters for chocolate chips. The next day she made the cakes with a friend (using our independent cookery book – see Appendix A).

> Cooking is an activity that will motivate and engage nearly all children. This motivation can lead to art, design, writing, maths, physical challenge and great fun, as well as delicious food. No wonder it occurs almost every day in our class!

Dancing

Diloo had managed to use the school digital camera to make a video clip of herself dancing with her sister. This led to much music-making and dancing in the garden.

Musical instruments are available in the garden, too, and these are often used to accompany the music when a CD is playing in the garden.

Music-making

Lia had photos of herself playing a keyboard at home. We then brought a keyboard to class and she played 'Old MacDonald', and tried to teach the others.

Role play and design

Liam had a photo of himself eating a burger and drinking a milkshake on the bus. Later that day, a bus was built in the garden, and then several children made themselves a meal to eat on it.

All the equipment for large-scale construction is stored outdoors and available for use all the time.

Initial stimulus provided by staff

When we were setting up the garden at the start of term, we hid some clay faces in the trees and it is only this week that the children have spotted these. This caused great excitement and (in a few children) fear.

It is unusual for us to set up a situation like this. However, I found these faces captivating and knew that the children would love them too. I had no idea what would result from this initial stimulus with children taking their learning in numerous directions.

Once they got over the initial shock, they started to look for more faces and found a second one. Some children then drew their own scary faces to stick on the trees. One child wanted to go and look at all the trees in the school grounds and many others went along too. Eventually the children found a third face on a tree in the nursery garden, but none on the junior field. Liam then wanted to make a face for the juniors, which he did with clay. A few days later the clay faces had been fired and so the children painted them with acrylics and we fixed them to trees on the junior field.

We pushed paper clips into the clay before it was fired and this made the pieces easy to attach to the trees with nails.

Today, Serif wanted to make a cake and asked me to help him write a shopping list. He then said, 'Can we go to the shop now to buy the ingredients for the cakes?' – an amazing sentence from this child! Thirteen other children went along too.

At the home visit, parents sign a form allowing us to take the children out into the local area. This means that we can respond immediately to such requests.

The next day, Serif made his cake. The 'scary face' theme (from the trees) is ongoing and was seen in the cake too!

Children design and then make their cake.

Sewing

The sewing box was used for the first time today. I was embroidering a name in a sweatshirt and several children were curious. I pointed out the sewing box and immediately three children started work on the binka with very satisfying results.

Given the opportunity, young children can sew safely and confidently.

Independent, sustained play

I observed a group of girls today who were role playing for nearly an hour – acting out a sleep-over. It was great to see this group gel. There were three girls from our nursery and three that were new to the school. No adult intervention was needed the whole time.

This is a lovely example of the outcome of the 'teaching' from September. These girls were able to co-operate, negotiate and use the resources successfully. They were totally absorbed in the game, using their initiative to improvise props, costumes and dialogue for their adventure.

The first half-term in any Early Years setting is exhausting and the break at the end of October is very welcome. This year the staff had worked hard to ensure that the children were settled and happy, with the majority staying all day.

3 | November

In this chapter I talk briefly about school dinners and our approach to weapon play, and I also explain how and why we assess levels of involvement. In the environment section, I describe the graphics areas indoors and outside and also large-scale construction outdoors. The diary section for this month contains just a few of the events that occurred. From literally hundreds of activities I have included those where a single 'theme' was continued over a sustained period.

NOVEMBER: TO DO LIST
- Continue with the first cycle of focus groups.
- Encourage children to try new foods.
- Discuss and agree on an approach to weapon play.
- Assess levels of involvement and seek help if needed.

School dinners

Like many people, I find the increasing numbers of obese children quite frightening. At school, we are in a position to educate children about their diet in a very real way – by sitting with them, eating with them, talking to them about their food and modelling healthy eating. We explain to each family at the home visit that everyone in the Reception class has school dinners, including the teachers. When concerns are expressed about 'fussy eaters', we reassure parents that once sitting with their friends the children will often eat things they have never touched at home. The majority of our children are entitled to free school meals and working parents are more than happy to be relieved of the chore of making a packed lunch. It still amazes me that children ask 'What is that?' – pointing to a potato! They have only ever seen them in chip form. We encourage the children to taste new foods and praise them when they do.

There are always a few children who find this challenging and nag their parents to have packed lunch. At this point I will discuss the idea with the family and stress that they need to persevere for as long as possible and that the long-term benefits will be worthwhile. Each year we only have one or two children who switch to packed lunch. In terms of life skills, eating a healthy diet has to be one of the most important.

Weapon play

Many children's television programmes and computer games are dominated by weapons and fighting. Inevitably, these themes enter the games played at school. This is one area where we have still to come to a clear agreement. I was brought up hearing the phrase 'familiarity breeds consent' and weapon play was banned. However, children will make weapons in secret if they are not able to make them openly, and then we cannot monitor the play effectively. At present, in De Bohun, we do not encourage the making of weapons, nor do we ban it. I make it very clear to the children that I do not want any weapon pointed at me and they all respect this. I also explain that it upsets me to see them pointing weapons at other children and that they should only point them at 'monsters', 'aliens' or 'baddies' etc. Children seem quite happy with this guideline but, as stated, this is an ongoing area of debate.

Assessing levels of involvement

The work of Ferre Laevers has made it possible to assess levels of involvement of individuals, groups and whole classes in an objective way. Laevers describes five levels of involvement. Although visitors to our school may be unaware of the relevant descriptors, they all comment on this aspect of the class with phrases such as 'They are all so calm and busy' or 'No-one is charging around'. This assessment of the class is actually an assessment of the levels of involvement being displayed.

It is just as easy, in some settings, to see very low-level involvement, and this should set alarm bells ringing. If the majority of children are not involved, then the provision is not meeting their needs. The team needs to reflect, review and amend what is on offer.

With regard to individual children, each one should be engaged and enthusiastic in their pursuits (for most of the time). If they are not, there are two possible reasons: either the provision is not meeting their needs, or there is an emotional problem that means the child is not able to relax and become absorbed in an activity.

Children operate at their highest level when totally absorbed in an activity – so involved that they do not hear you when you call their name. The child who is nervous, watchful or lethargic is unable to reach this level of involvement and therefore unable to achieve their full potential. This is an incredibly complex area and each year we have children in our class who cause concern in this way. Initially, we amend the provision to try to capture their interest and imagination. However, if the problem is actually outside school, or an emotional problem within the child, then outside help may be needed and must be sought. Again, this is beyond the remit of this book but is another source of stress and concern for all teachers.

Assessing these levels, however, is an important first step to take if you have concerns about a particular child or group. Knowing what to do about it is far more difficult. Do not, however, ignore the problem. Discuss the issues, ask for advice and insist on help.

Setting up the environment

Graphics: indoors and outdoors

Mark-making occurs everywhere: writing shopping lists, drawing maps, producing 2D artwork in the creative area, running a finger through the sand, making indentations in the play dough, using the mouse to draw on the PC, painting on the playground with water etc.

Indoors we have one area of the room that has all the resources necessary for graphics. It is an area that is generally quiet, but near to the creative area so that children feel able to combine the use of the resources.

The graphics provision is duplicated outdoors.

Beside the table is a unit with trays labelled with words and a photo of the contents. These units are not ideal since the children cannot see what is inside. The trays contain a variety of items:

- white plain paper
- coloured paper
- lined paper
- card
- envelopes
- booklets (for children to write in)
- exercise books
- whiteboards and marker pens
- magnetic letters
- alphabet cards
- themed paper.

Nearby is a string and clothes pegs and the children can peg up unfinished work to keep it safe, as well as finished pieces for display. Stories are also kept here before being read to the class and acted out (see December).

The children peg up their on-going work or finished pieces for safe-keeping.

Storage for mark–making implements is often problematic. Educational catalogues are not the only place to find storage solutions!

A few of the family photos can be seen on top of the storage unit.

The pots in this photo are great (from IKEA) – children remove one item or the whole pot and put it on the table. The children have real choices from a selection of quality materials. These pots contain the following, but the possibilities are endless:

- glue sticks
- scissors
- large crayons

- thin felt pens
- thick felt pens
- coloured pencils
- HB pencils
- sharpeners
- paper clips
- rubbers
- biros and gel pens
- thin crayons
- highlighter pens.

Nearby we have rulers, staplers, Sellotape, masking tape and phonic cards.

The blue cards between the pots are attached with Velcro so that the children can remove these and replace them with ease. There is a card for each child with their name and photo. The children use these to write their friends' names. On discovering that the adults did not have a name card, some children drew the adults and added their names to a card. They then insisted that these were laminated and added to the display.

Nearby is an alphabet frieze with pictures painted by children and outlined by an adult. We have photocopied these and used them to make our phonic cards.

The majority of this provision is replicated in the garden, including the alphabet frieze, the mark-making implements and paper. Resources outside are stored on an old bookshelf, which is covered with a tarpaulin at night. The shelving is next to a table and chairs, and, in addition, there are two enormous whiteboards (rejects from the juniors). We also have a gigantic blackboard, made with marine plywood and painted with blackboard paint.

The appropriate whiteboard pens are attached with Velcro near the board.

All resources are checked, tidied and restocked on a daily basis.

Large-scale construction outdoors

Some resources don't cost anything!

The large wooden blocks, produced by Community Playthings, are the most expensive items we have. However, they are one of the most valuable too (in terms of play value). They are stored in a shed that is open each day (when it's not raining) and this has been placed near to a large, clear area and beside other construction materials. You will see numerous examples of their use in this book and in most cases they are combined with other objects. The resources are listed below, but the possibilities are endless. I often find things at the side of the road and bring them to school (much to the amazement of my family). This is how we got the dismantled cot, the car bumper, the number-plates and the hub caps! Keep an eye on skips too – they are a wonderful source of free resources.

- Community Playthings blocks
- cot sides (great for barriers and fencing)
- car bumper, tyres, number-plates and hub caps
- bread trays
- milk crates
- old booster seats
- ropes
- old shower hoses
- cones
- fabric (stored in a salt bin)
- carpet pieces
- planks and a ladder
- broom handles
- clothes pegs

Den building with fabric, string and pegs.

In numerous settings, I have seen expensive, fixed equipment, the appeal of which is short-lived, and then the equipment is abandoned. It is better to have resources that allow children to build an infinite number of things themselves – submarines, caravans, motorbikes – and at a fraction of the cost.

Diary extracts: examples of development and learning

WHAT TO LOOK OUT FOR
- Generally high levels of involvement.
- Children enjoying new foods at school.
- Sustained involvement over longer periods of time.
- Children confident to initiate challenging activities.

Each month, some themes develop over periods of time. The diary extracts below are examples of such events from November.

Pizzas

One focus child this week brought in photos showing herself at a restaurant with her family. Another parent wrote that her child loved pizza – we therefore set up a pizza restaurant in the role play area. The pizza restaurant is very popular and several children have suggested making real pizzas. They set about 'writing' what toppings they would like. These were bought and the real pizzas were made and shared with the whole class. Many children tasted green pepper for the first time.

It was noticeable how willing the children were to try the new toppings on the pizzas. All the Reception children are still having school dinners, and all but one are eating really well. The pizza restaurant was used for about two weeks and then the interest switched to doctors, and a surgery was set up (see Chapter 6 for role play details).

Bridges

Some children asked an adult to read 'Where the Wild Things Are'. This led to several children role playing 'monster' games. The children then wanted to go looking for monsters in the school grounds. When they found the pond, some suggested that the monster was living under the water. Back in the garden the children used two mats as the pond and built bridges to walk on and look for the monsters.

After several collisions on the bridges, some children added arrows to show which direction the bridges were to be used. This game was repeated several times over a period of a few days.

Paper, pens and tape etc. are available outdoors and this facilitates the production of signs, labels and, in this case, arrows.

A few days later, there was a giant puddle in the playground. Several children were playing in and around the puddle and then some children decided to join some rubber matting squares together to make a bridge.

Once the bridge was in place, the middle section was in fact 'floating' on the puddle. One child walked slowly across, the bridge went down and the water flowed over it. Another boy ran over it and found that his feet stayed dry if he ran fast enough. Many children then had a turn at running over the 'wibbly wobbly bridge'.

The children discovered that their feet stayed dry if they ran quickly so that the bridge didn't sink.

The bridge theme continued later in the week – the puddle had gone but a group built a bridge with blocks. Some children extended this by balancing objects on their head while they walked over the bridge.

> The events that developed around the theme of bridges were imaginative, ambitious and exciting. I doubt if an adult could have planned such a valuable series of lessons – another reason to let the children take the lead.

Dragons and chocolate cake

The storywriting continues to be popular (see Chapter 4). This week, Melanie, one of the focus children, became involved for the first time. Early in the week she was making chocolate cake in the sand pit 'for the dragon – to make it be nice'.

Children are fascinated by the activity of combining water and sand.

She then painted a picture of two dragons and, with encouragement, she dictated the story about them as follows:

> The dragons scare someone. They fly away and we see a pumpkin. We make it for the dragons. It's a chocolate cake. When we see the dragon we throw the chocolate cake. They eat it. They got nice. Then they get no more fire on us.

The next day she made chocolate cake and was taught how to follow the recipe and use the balance accurately. At the end of the day, a group, including Melanie, acted out her story and then everyone had a piece of cake.

> This is a lovely example of how all areas of development have been covered without any need to coax or persuade the child to participate. She had a wonderful week and was supported in taking the 'next steps' in her learning.

Dancing

There is a large group of children who love dancing in this class, and a mum volunteered to make us some dancing skirts and waistcoats. These arrived and caused great excitement. The girls then asked for 'ballet music' and we learnt that two of them go to ballet lessons. Our student, Lorna, then offered to demonstrate Irish dancing and the children joined in, copying the steps with care.

Irish dancing.

One girl then said she did Greek dancing and so we put on Zorba and the children danced to this.

I often talk to practitioners who are worried about introducing 'dance' in their settings because they do not feel confident to dance themselves. Many children love to dance. Put on the music and let them teach the class.

A free gift

Today I got a phone call from a friend who was trying to 'give away' a caravan! Needless to say I jumped at the opportunity to have this in our garden, and thankfully the Head has agreed and it is to be delivered next week.

The caravan was brought into the garden and pushed into position.

The children were very excited. They watched as it was manoeuvred and they moved logs to put under it for stability. The rest of the day was spent with various groups in and out of the caravan, exploring, adding resources and agreeing behaviours. The table was broken within minutes! I took the locks off the toilet cubicle because several children were locking other children in there. Everyone agreed that it was not a place for running or loud games. One girl made a television, complete with DVD player and remote control. I heard several children commenting, 'Turn the sound up a bit!'

Would you know that this TV is in fact a cardboard box? Look at the expressions on the faces of these children. Note one boy has leaned over to turn up the volume!

At one end of the caravan there is a full-size cooker, sink and fridge. Children are rarely allowed to touch a real cooker, and the language and play was extremely realistic as a result. Some clothes were put in the wardrobe, books on the shelves, and pencils and paper in the drawers. One child decided that the caravan needed a doorbell, and this was easily resolved with a bottle top taped into place on the side of the caravan.

> It would have been easy to refuse the offer of a caravan because of perceived problems and 'risks'. The children would have been very disappointed. Whenever an exciting opportunity is on offer, assess the problems carefully and go ahead if at all possible. The extra effort is always worthwhile in terms of the learning and development, engagement and fun.

November can be one of the hardest months in school – cold, wet and dark. It is also one of the few months in the school year when there is no break at all. However, although the staff and children were very tired, these diary extracts show that we had an exciting and eventful month, much of which was spent outdoors.

4 December

In this chapter I discuss culture and religion, describe work done with one focus child and explain story scribing. The environment section includes our snack table, maths opportunities and the woodwork bench. The diary section gives numerous activities that were absorbing and valuable at the time but did not lead to any major projects or last very long. We do not try to develop everything – sometimes activities are completed and we are satisfied with the result, even if achieved in a short time. It is not possible to pursue everything.

DECEMBER: TO DO LIST

- Complete first cycle of focus children.
- Complete first cycle of parent meetings.
- Update childrens' individual folders.
- Discuss religious festivities with team and decide how to proceed.
- Organise end-of-term party (if you wish).
- Be flexible and join whole-school activities if appropriate.

Culture and religion

December brings dilemmas for teachers in all schools. How appropriate is it to teach very young children about any specific religion? With our way of working, there are opportunities for cultural and religious events to be relayed to the class in a spontaneous and more meaningful way. Children relate their own experiences from home and other children listen and respond in an atmosphere of trust. For example, Jas made firework pictures because of Diwali and others joined her in this activity. We have a wide-ranging mix of languages, cultures and beliefs in De Bohun (18 different first languages in the class this year). Our class has a culture of its own – a culture where interest, respect and acceptance of others are modelled by staff and adopted by the children. As you read this chapter, you will see other examples of this complex issue.

Working with a focus child

In order to clarify our 'spontaneous' approach to planning, I have included below a diary extract describing some events that emerged for one focus child, Dahir. When writing up the 'learning journey', all six areas of learning were covered with ease. The adult interventions allowed Dahir to take 'next steps' in numerous areas. The development of language is clear, but he also held a worm, spoke to an adult and used blocks as a unit of measurement etc. He showed high-level involvement and had memorable experiences.

The traditional cycle of 'observation, assessment and planning' can be spread over days or weeks, but this is not necessary. It is far more effective (in terms of development and learning) when the observation and assessment lead to an activity immediately, as seen here.

On Tuesday Dahir found a worm and was very excited. He was reluctant to touch the worm, saying 'Dirty, mummy say dirty'. After I held it, he was willing to let it crawl on his hand, but dropped it when it went up his sleeve! The next day he was reading a book about snakes. I sat down next to him and he was very keen to show me the pictures. He then started to talk about the pictures using two- or three-word phrases – 'Snake eat frog', etc. I remembered that we had been given two snake skins by a parent. I got the bag out and let Dahir explore what was inside. He was amazed and excited. At one point he said, 'Snake sleeping?' I pointed to my skin and said, 'Snake skin – no snake'. He then got the skins out and placed them on the floor, lay down next to them and made me lie down too. One of them was longer than me!

Dahir is still holding the reference book while examining the snake skin.

I then encouraged Dahir to use community blocks as a unit to measure the snakes. Several children joined the activity and there was a lot of counting and recounting before it was established that the longer snake was 14 blocks long and the shorter one was 11. After a while, Dahir approached me and said, 'Snake outside?' He had never verbalised a request to me before. I said, 'Yes, you can take the snake outside'. I showed him how to carry it around his neck. Once outside, he pointed to a tree and then said 'camera', and took a photo of the snake in the tree.

Dahir was so captivated by the snake skin that he overcame his nerves and spoke to an adult to ask for something.

When children are engaged in this way, it is a perfect opportunity to develop their **language skills**. At many points during this period with Dahir, I commented on what I saw or thought, allowing him to hear words and phrases in context. I also modelled correct phrases. For example, when Dahir said 'camera?', I replied, 'Yes, you can have the camera'. Thus he heard the correct phrase without his error being explicitly pointed out.

The cycle of **'observation – assessment – planning – observation'** continued during the week for Dahir, but with gaps of only a few minutes between each phase of the cycle. **There is great potential for development through current fascinations and this may be missed if the introduction of an activity is delayed until the following week.**

Story scribing

I had often spent time scribing stories for the children, but the work of Vivian Gussin Paley inspired me to encourage the children to act out those stories. Early in the autumn term we actively seek out children who are keen to do this. They dictate their story to an adult and it is recorded exactly as it is told (without any correction of the grammar etc.). We do tend to limit the length of the stories to one page, purely for time-management reasons. Once the story is finished, the child will often want to illustrate it, and then it is pegged up near the graphics table for safe-keeping. During a carpet session, the children sit in a semicircle, to create a 'stage', an adult selects children to be the characters in the story (usually including the author) and they act out the story as the adult reads. Once the other children see the performance they are then keen to write their own stories, and then the activity spirals, with stories being dictated and acted on a daily basis. By December this year, the acting was improving, with the children becoming more expressive in their actions and words.

The group acts out the story as it is read by an adult.

This activity is valuable in so many ways. The desire to dictate a story encourages all children to extend their language skills. They also develop creatively by making up the story and then acting it out. Performing as part of a group takes the pressure off individuals and helps some children become more confident in front of an audience. While dictating their story, the children watch an adult writing, making the process and purpose of writing very clear.

In a Reception class, it is simple to take this process further. I make sure I read back what is written at intervals to ensure that it makes sense and so that the child can follow on with the next part of the story. This is a good way of modelling the skill of scanning and checking writing. I say each word as I write, point out that I need to leave gaps and show where to add full stops. Thus they realise that each group of letters makes up a word and groups of words make sentences. In many cases, the children want their friends to be characters in the story and when a name crops up I ask, 'Do you want to write that bit?' They are often keen to do so, run off to get the appropriate name card and copy it into the story.

I sound out some words as I write, giving the child the chance to hear segmented words. I may ask, for example, 'cat – what sounds can you hear in cat?' The child may just give the initial sound or may give all three sounds. We know the children very well and are able to judge which children are ready for this.

Eventually, with some children, when it comes to words that are phonetically correct, or common words, such as 'the', I might say, 'Oh, would you like to write that word?' We discuss the sounds needed, they take the pen and write the word. All such attempts are praised and errors are never corrected. We want the children to see themselves as writers and any suggestion that their attempt is lacking could put them off writing completely. Gradually, some children take the pen more and more, until eventually they are writing complete phrases.

This month saw two boys writing their own stories. At this point in the year, the writing was not legible by an adult. However, the boys knew that their marks on the paper told their stories. They read them to the class while a group acted them out.

A group of children acted out the story as it was 'read' by the author!

The activity of scribing in this way has a huge impact on the writing ability of the children. Those who are ready and keen to write do so with ease, producing stories, books and captions that are meaningful and relevant to them.

Setting up the environment

Snack table indoors

Snacks and drinks are available all day.

It is difficult to focus when thirsty or hungry. We try to ensure that this is not a problem. Our snack table is in use all day. There are five seats at a round table with milk and water to drink. There are mugs available, and, once used, the children place these in a bowl to be washed. We have fruit and some salad and vegetables depending what has been delivered as part of the fruit scheme. We also have toast available at the start of the day (left over from the Breakfast Club). There are chopping boards and knives for the children to use if they wish. There are usually children at this table at all times of the day. They sit and chat, drink and eat. It is a relaxed, sociable area and adults join the group for a snack too.

Maths opportunities indoors and outside

We do not have a specific maths area since maths is happening in all areas: in the play dough equipment, there are shaped cutters, scales for balancing and cutlery to make into sets. Children discuss how many cookies have been cut, what shape they are and how much they are going to cost to sell. In the water play equipment, there are measuring jugs and containers of various shapes and sizes. We discuss how many stones it will take to sink a boat, or which syringe can fire the water the furthest. At the snack table there are knives to cut fruit into halves or quarters and discussions about how many strawberries each child should have. In the large construction area outdoors, the models are often symmetrical, the cars have the correct number of wheels and arrows are added to obstacle courses to indicate direction.

Note the salt bins behind this model – fantastic for storage.

In the 'jungle', the children decide how high up the trees they should climb, count to given numbers when playing hide-and-seek and look at patterns on the leaves. The woodwork bench involves consideration of shape, size and angle as well as counting wheels for vehicles etc. The Creative Cascade set involves concepts of higher and lower to get an effective slope. The examples are endless.

There are numbers displayed around the classroom and garden, and the number line featuring photos of the children is particularly popular.

Indoors there are trays containing number puzzles, card games, lotto and simple board games as well as containers of objects to sort and count. Adult interactions lead to mathematical concepts being extended or commentated upon. For example, the adult may encourage children to keep score in their tennis match or to aim the football at numbers chalked on the wall. A defined maths area would imply that this is where maths is done. That would not only be restrictive; it would also give the wrong message. We want the children to see maths as a tool to use everywhere and this is what we model and encourage.

The woodwork bench outdoors

Although the woodwork bench can only be used by two children at a time, it is a fantastic resource leading to development in numerous areas and engaging children who may have never demonstrated high levels of involvement. Benefits include development of hand–eye co-ordination, strength in hand and arm muscles, design and planning, use of tools, construction techniques, understanding of the quality of materials, perseverance, and pride in their achievements. Many practitioners are worried about accidents and this prevents them pursuing this activity. At De Bohun, we insist that the children have 'two hands on the saw'. This ensures that the wood is in the vice to be cut. We have never had a child injured with a saw. The children sometimes hit their fingers with the hammer but do not do any serious damage. No-one has ever hit anyone else with a hammer. The perceived risks are greater than the actual risks – it is definitely worthwhile.

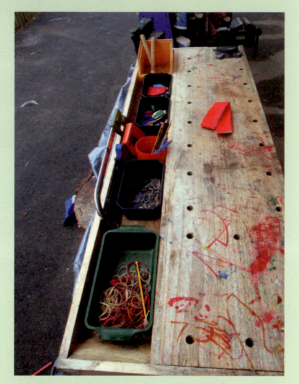

Tools and resources neatly stored.

The main reason the woodwork bench is outdoors is because it is noisy and would disrupt the generally calm atmosphere indoors. It is placed near the door so staff from inside and outside can keep an eye on it. After the initial training period, we do not have an adult at the work bench unless a child requests help or when a new child joins the class.

We have an adult work bench with the legs sawn off to make it the right height – cheaper than buying through an educational catalogue. There are two vices, hammers, saws (large hacksaws with fine teeth are best) and a battery-operated sander. We have also had a drill, but the children seem to remove and lose the drill bits on a daily basis. On the bench are pots containing nails, various bottle tops, corks, elastic bands, pens and off-cuts of coloured corroflute. The children also combine resources from other areas – e.g. fabric for a bed. The wood is stored on an old bookshelf beside the bench. I get the wood from a local carpenter who keeps all his off-cuts. He is delighted to know that they are being put to good use. Some DIY stores will also give off-cuts to schools. Newsletters making requests to parents can be productive too. Both the bookshelf and the work bench have tarpaulin stapled on to the back of them and this is pulled over at the end of each day and secured with a hoop of elasticated rope. Once again – no need for time to set up in the morning – just remove the tarpaulin and the work bench is ready to use.

Diary extracts: examples of development and learning

WHAT TO LOOK OUT FOR

- Progress seen in all children in most areas.
- Clear understanding of the process of 'reading'.
- Children more confident when acting out stories.
- Children beginning to see themselves as 'writers'.

The extracts below describe generally short events, most of which had no follow-up activity. In each case, they could have been extended, but there are just not enough hours in the day. A few activities show how cultural events impact on the class.

Eid and Christmas

Two of the focus children had pictures of presents being opened as part of Eid celebrations.

This is a good example of an event occurring (presents for Eid), which then allowed a discussion of presents in general and who receives them and when. The children were quick to point out the similarity with Christmas.

Head scarves

Everyone was wrapped up well against the cold and Hanan commented on how Jacqui looked like her when she put her scarf up on her head.

This simple comment led to a discussion about who wears head scarves and why. Hanan said her scarf was to keep her warm! This sort of discussion allows the children to discuss their culture in their own terms.

Upper-body strength

Several children who found the rope bridge impossible at the start of the year are now able to go right across it. The improved upper-body strength means that these same children are now keen to have a go at writing at least one or two letters from their names.

Gross motor skill development precedes fine motor control.

Finding a hedgehog

The highlight of today was finding a hedgehog in the garden. We kept it in a box for a while so that all the children could look at it. We fed it some of the roast lamb from lunch – which it loved. Dahir, in particular, was amazed and thrilled to see this little creature. Liam and Serif then decided to draw the hedgehog.

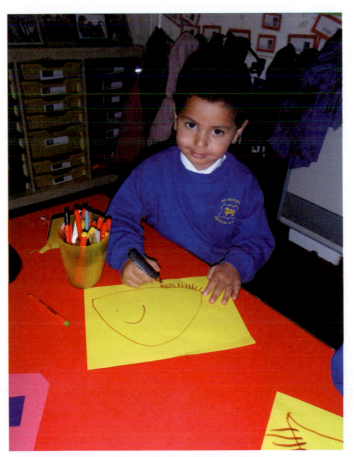

The workshop set-up means that children are able to access paper and pens independently whenever they need them.

Goldilocks

Goldilocks has become popular. One group was on the carpet (independently of an adult) with one child reading the story and a few others acting it out. I suggested they find some resources – chairs, bowls etc. – which they did. I then stood back and watched. Jessica read the story and the others acted it out.

The children see themselves as 'readers' and value reading as a source of pleasure and information.

The actors used appropriate voices and the narrator used the traditional phrases from the story. Throughout the afternoon the group on the carpet changed, with different children joining and leaving. No adult intervention was needed – they organised themselves with about eight different children having a turn at 'reading' and with the story being repeated and acted eight or more times.

Year 2 nativity play

We took the class in to watch the Year 2 nativity play. This was the first time the children had sat in a 'whole-school' event. It was only 20 minutes long and they sat mesmerised.

> Because the children are not forced to sit through assemblies on a daily basis, this experience was a novelty to them. Sitting in the large hall, glimpsing their older siblings and with a show to watch, the activity was engaging and appropriate.

Christmas

Christmas has arrived in the classroom – the tree is up and there is even a mini tree in the caravan! Alison encouraged the children to make a card and to write inside. Lots of children are bringing cards for the class.

Should we be making Christmas cards? This is one of the activities that has caused discussion amongst the team. Eventually it was agreed to set up the activity and the children had the option to make a card if they so wished. Many of the team are parents and still treasure the cards that their children brought home from their Reception class. Other discussions concern the tree – should we have one or not? The staff and children love the tree and coloured lights, and so the tree was put up in the class. I am sure there will be more debate about this next year.

Party day

Today the children came to school in party clothes and were very excited. We gave the children the chance to make party hats in the morning and most did so. We decided to end the morning session early as the children were so excited. We put on the film 'The Snowman' and they sat mesmerised for 30 minutes. Most had never seen the film. After lunch we played some party games, had food, and then Santa arrived with a present (a hand-held hoover – perfect for the caravan and home corner).

Games, food and presents – appealing to all children.

Hairdressing

Today some girls started to do Alison's hair in the home corner. The group was keen to help set up a hairdressers in the role play area. We included an appointment book with the days of the week written at the top for the children to look at and copy if they wish. It also has numbers up to 12, so that the children can select an appointment time and write this in the book too.

The children are never told to write — they use writing in their play, just as they use a telephone or a hat — it makes their game more realistic.

Santa, Eid, Christmas and parties — all huge areas of contention and debate. At our school, the debate goes on, and I think that is what is important. Discuss, review and reflect on events. At De Bohun, every child had a varied, interesting and fun month and no child felt excluded or uncomfortable.

5 January

In this chapter I will describe the role of the adult, briefly discuss risk assessment and look at fluctuating pupil numbers. Two areas of the environment are described: the sand area indoors and physical challenge outdoors. Apart from activities related to the snow, the diary also includes the introduction of some more formal phonics teaching as well as some ambitious child-initiated learning.

JANUARY: TO DO LIST

- Spend time settling the children back into the routines and expectations after the holiday.
- Respond to the weather creatively.
- Introduce Phase Two phonics.
- Review all aspects of the provision and amend where necessary.
- Review special needs children and create new targets.
- Start second cycle of focus groups.
- Start second cycle of parent meetings.
- Moderate Foundation Stage Profiles with other members of staff.
- Resist pressure (from whatever source) for a more formal curriculum.

Adults roles

When a class is run as a workshop, with children accessing resources and activities independently, it is not possible for the teacher to know about everything that is happening. Some practitioners find this concerning, asking questions such as:

'How do you know who can do what?'
'How do you know who has accessed any maths today?'
'How do they learn to write if you don't make them do it?'
'What if a child never comes out of the sand pit?'

It is difficult for such practitioners to 'let go' and to hand over control to the children. Practitioners need to take a leap of faith and believe in the natural curiosity and desire to learn that all children have. Once they do so, they will see that what we actually **teach** children is only a tiny part of what they actually **learn.** The adult takes on a very different role in such a set-up. The adult is vital in establishing the environment and atmosphere that allows the child to explore. The adult is essential to help the child who is trying to do something where maybe just one step in the process is slightly beyond their capability at present.

In the table below, I have listed a sample of the child-initiated activities I saw today. I have then listed the roles in which I saw adults engaging with these children, and the third list shows adult roles that were independent of the children.

Child-initiated activities	Link between child and adult	Adult roles (O/PH = observations/ photographs)
experimenting with magnets	conversation	O/PH
building an obstacle course in the garden	conversation, helping as requested	O/PH, risk assessment
story writing	conversation, scribing, modelling, helping as requested	re-stocking, O/PH
writing on the chalk board		O/PH
bookmaking	conversation, scribing, helping as requested	re-stocking, O/PH
dressmaking – for children and for dolls	conversation, helping as requested – holding fabric, threading needles	re-stocking, O/PH
hairdressing	conversation, modelling	O/PH
listening to story tapes,		O/PH
water play		re-stocking, O/PH
mixing mud and water in saucepans	conversation	
model making – with recycled materials		re-stocking, O/PH
measuring self against a puzzle	conversation, modelling	O/PH
computers – accessing the internet and playing number games	conversation	O/PH
role play in the caravan		
setting up the Brio train set	conversation	O/PH
cutting old greetings cards and using to make new cards	conversation, helping as requested – scribing messages, phonics	re-stocking, O/PH
reading in a small group		O/PH
climbing on the rope ladder and bridge		O/PH risk assessment
feeding the guinea pigs	conversation, helping as requested, modelling	O/PH risk assessment
using the Creative Cascade set for cars		
dancing to number songs played on the IWB		
group playing with large puppets	modelling	O/PH
children reading books to the puppets		O/PH
group at snack table	conversation	re-stocking, O/PH

Figure 5.1 Adult roles

In each case, where you see the word 'conversation', this could involve questioning, clarifying, narrating, listening, encouraging and explaining – i.e. sustained shared thinking, which may help the child take the 'next step' in their learning.

Instead of believing that the children will learn less when a class is run in this way, practitioners soon realise that the children have so many more choices and therefore so many more opportunities to learn.

In order to be as responsive and flexible as possible, we do not have rotas for the staff. Every adult needs to be willing to move between activities, indoors and out according to the needs of the situation.

Risk assessment

Risk assessment has become a huge issue in all settings. Unfortunately, it has led to many activities being stopped for fear of accidents and possible legal consequences. I heard this week of a school where the staff had put up rope swings, which the children loved and were using well, until the head teacher came out and cut them down! I know of another setting where the children had a wonderful 'jungle' area in the bushes until one child's face got scratched. All the bushes were removed the next week! Children learn how to move through bushes by moving through bushes. They learn how to hold on tightly to a rope by doing just that. Hard playgrounds cause the most injuries in schools – with children tripping and falling regularly. For some reason this is accepted, but being scratched by a bush is not. There is no logic to this.

We do have accidents in our garden, but we are constantly monitoring the activities (as the table above shows). If an adult sees something dangerous, we discuss it with the children and come to an agreement. Thus the trees have recently had ribbons tied on them to indicate the limit to which the children can climb. No-one is allowed to push the wagon; it must only be pulled so that the child at the front is in control. Each day brings new activities and each activity is assessed at the time. It is a continuous process.

When we take groups out of school, the risk assessment is more challenging because we are not in control of the environment. Also, no matter how carefully you plan, it is impossible to think of every eventuality.

Some points need to be considered on every occasion when taking a group out (see Figure 5.2).

Expect the unexpected and be alert at all times. Outings are exhausting for this reason – you cannot relax for a second. Don't be frightened into avoiding outings – the benefits are well worthwhile.

New children joining the class

In some schools, the 30 children that start in September are still there the following July, but this is not always the case. We have one of the highest mobility rates in our borough and this brings new challenges. We have children leaving and joining our class every month. This constant mobility creates a great deal of extra work for staff – visits, settling, setting up folders, peg labels etc.

A new girl, Alisha, started this term. It is very interesting to see a new child in the well-established group. At one point she was with a group digging the snow and said to an adult nearby, 'They nearly hit me with that spade'. The adult said, 'You need to speak to the children and say "be careful please"'. She looked horrified and stomped away from the group and stood at a distance with her arms folded, scowling. She clearly expected

Ratio of adults to children	(Dependent on type of outing)
Part-time staff	(Will they be able to work for the duration of the outing?)
Part-time children	(Will they be able to participate in the whole outing?)
Other duties that staff may have at school	(Arrange cover)
Weather	(Obvious considerations)
Safest route/transport	(If walking – which is the quietest route? Public transport – ensure transport staff are available to help. Coaches – ensure they have seat belts)
Yellow jackets for staff	(These make the traffic slow down a little)
Mobile phones	(A fantastic resource when something goes wrong)
Change of clothes	(In case of accidents)
First-aid kit	
Inhalers	
Crossing roads	(We always actually stop the traffic – the yellow jackets help with this too)
Hand-washing	(If touching animals)
Toilets	(Where are they? Plan times to take the whole group.)
Food and drink	(How to carry it and what to take).

Figure 5.2 Risk assessment for outings

the adult to sort this problem out for her. After a few minutes, when no-one had paid her any attention, she rejoined the group. She had about five episodes like this during the course of the day. By the end of the day, she was beginning to say the phrases that were modelled to her by the staff. Over the course of the next few weeks, she learnt to negotiate and express her feelings. She became happy and relaxed in the class.

Setting up the environment

January is often freezing, and for some staff the cold weather is a real challenge – but not for the children. We still have the door open all day. We have purchased plastic strips, as used in warehouses, which hang in the doorway to keep the cold out of the classroom.

Sand play indoors

Unlike the outdoor sand area, the indoor sand play needs to be kept tidy to a certain extent. We keep this sand dry and have coloured sand to make it attractive and appealing. The resources to use in the sand are placed nearby, easily accessible in labelled containers. Children sometimes transport resources from other areas, if appropriate. The resources include the following, but there are numerous possibilities:

Clear labels mean children can tidy up easily.

- sand wheel
- sieves
- stones
- shells
- sticks
- spades and forks
- plastic cups and saucers
- cutlery
- plastic animals
- toy people
- cars and diggers
- dustpan and brush.

As with any area in the class, once a child has finished playing, they are encouraged to put resources away and then to sweep the floor.

Physical challenge outdoors

The majority of our children do not have access to a garden at home. Many are not taken to parks or playgrounds on a regular basis. Opportunities for physical challenge are important for all children and absolutely vital where this is not available outside school. We are very lucky that our head teacher encourages children to be physically active, with appropriate risk-taking.

Gross motor skills are developed in numerous ways (sand play outdoors and wood-work are described in other chapters). We offer the usual PE equipment as well as the following:

- rope swing
- rope bridge
- rope ladder
- tree climbing
- A-frames, ladders, planks and pole
- trikes
- go-kart
- wagons to pull
- scooter
- two-wheeler bikes
- football
- tennis
- hoppers
- skipping ropes
- hoola hoops
- Z-bugs
- ribbons on sticks
- monkey bars
- slopes.

This child has added crates to launch from, resulting in an extra high swing!

A rope bridge is easy to set up between two trees or pillars.

Wheeled toys are available for the first hour each day in the infant playground but not in the garden. In this way, the bikes do not dominate the garden or disrupt activities there (as is often the case with wheeled toys in a garden). We also have two-wheeler bikes, and by the end of the year more than half the class can ride these. We have removed the pedals from two of the bikes and this allows the children to practise getting their balance before progressing to the use of pedals.

Children have to wear helmets on the two-wheeled bikes.

There is a 'road' marked on the playground and we use cones with photos of each toy as 'bike stops'. For example, if a child wants a turn on the go-kart, they wait at the cone with the photo of the go-kart on it. The children go round the road once and return to the stop. If no-one is waiting for that toy, they can continue, but if someone else wants a turn, they get off and hand it over. This is one way to ensure that no adult is required to supervise the 'sharing' of bikes.

Storage

We store our bikes in two sheds in the infant playground and, once empty, the sheds become role play areas.

The PE equipment is stored in a salt bin from which the children select what they want.

These bins can be padlocked for security, if necessary.

Each time we make a decision about storage we ensure that the children can access it themselves. Whenever possible, it is kept in the area where it is used or else in a trolley that can be moved by the children. This removes the need for 'setting up' by adults and thus ensures that the equipment is more likely to be used regularly.

Diary extracts: examples of development and learning

WHAT TO LOOK OUT FOR
- Some regression initially in behaviour and speech in some children.
- Excitement and wonder in response to freezing weather.
- Greater interest in reading and writing.
- Increased awareness of phonics.
- Increased use of mathematical and scientific concepts in play.
- Improved speech amongst all children.
- Independence and creativity in all areas.
- Improvements in pencil control.
- Pressure from parents for a more formal curriculum.

The extracts below give examples of many of the items in the list above. The activities involving the snow dominated much of the month, but the spring term is often the time when we introduce some quick formal phonics teaching, and this is referred to as well.

Language development

Language development is becoming very evident now. For example, in November Alex drew a picture and an adult scribed for him:

Mummy, Baby, Daddy, Me.

This week he drew another picture and again the adult scribed:

Red Bat Man, Black Bat Man, Green Bat Man and Baby Bat Man and Mum go shopping. Shopping and then go to house. I go in house, give to fish eating. I say 'Hello Bat Man'. I play in Play Station. Play Station finished I making paint. I finished colour I play big computer. Bat Man said 'Bye!' The End.

> Children who are learning a new language will start to speak to their peers before they are confident enough to speak to adults. In a formal school setting, the opportunities for such speech are limited to the playtimes. However, in our class, the children are free to talk to each other for about 90 per cent of their time in school. The stories we scribe give one record of a child's ability in spoken English (see Chapter 4).

Phonic sessions

This week we did the first 'phase 2' phonic session with the whole class – 'a' for apple – and gave each child a card to take home. We sent home three cards during the week: t – a – p . Some children are able to blend and segment these already. We sent a note to parents to explain the programme (see Figure 5.9):

> Many of the children in the class are learning letter sounds as they need them. Each time they try to write something, an adult is on hand to help and to teach them which letters are used for which sounds. This also happens during story scribing sessions. However, we also follow the **'Letters and Sounds'** programme to ensure a structured series of lessons. The phonic sessions are only for ten minutes, three times a week. As each new sound is introduced, we teach the children **cued articulation** for that sound. This means that not only do the children hear and say sounds (connected to letters), but they also see and do a movement that actually helps their mouth go into the correct shape to form that sound. For some children, this helps with pronunciation, and for others it helps them to remember which letter makes which sound.

Reading books

Safia approached me today and said, 'My Mum said there is nothing in my bag and you need to put a book in there!'

Phonics

We have started on our phonics programme with the Reception children. The children will bring home new cards as they progress. Please keep the cards in the plastic wallet and return it to school each day.

Please look at the cards and help your child learn the letter **sounds**. (We do not learn the letter names at this time).

Try to think of objects that begin with that sound.

Play games with the cards – making three-letter words for your child to read (e.g. tap, pat) and asking them to try and make a word that you say.

If your child is keen to try and write the letters, that is fine, but please do not pressurise them to do this. If they do attempt this, please watch to ensure that they form the letters correctly.

Praise all their efforts and do not spend more than ten minutes each day on this activity – we are sure you have more interesting things to do!

Figure 5.3 Note to parents

Other parents have started asking when their child will have a 'reading book'. In most cases these are parents who have older children in the school. A few children are now demonstrating an awareness of phonics, word recognition and curiosity. At this point, some may benefit from the structure that a reading scheme offers. We will review this over the next few weeks.

Snow

After 3 'snow days', the school reopened, but we still have 10 cm of snow everywhere. The playground is not in use, but we gave the Reception children access to the garden for the whole day. Many children had not been out in the snow at home and were thrilled to be outdoors. Snowball fights started immediately. Instead of stopping this I brought the group together to discuss the rules. I started off by saying that I didn't want to play and that I didn't want to be hit by any snow. Another child said, 'I don't like the snow hitting my face'. The group agreed that the rules should be 'no throwing snow at faces' and 'only throw at people who want to play'. Once these rules were established, there were no problems and the group played independently for a long period.

If we give children the chance to create rules and boundaries, they often prove themselves more than capable of doing so. Why have a rule that says 'No snowball fights!' when it is possible to have simple rules that allow the fun to continue?

Another activity was 'sledging' on sandwich trays. (These trays arrived with sandwiches for the teachers on the INSET day.) This was a totally new experience for nearly all the children, and therefore adult input was essential. The slope was tiny and just thrilling enough for four-year-olds.

Some children persevered to develop the perfect sledging technique – sit down, wiggle, lie back, feet up.

When the slope needed more snow, the children used the wagon to transport it from the playground and field.

This wagon is used to transport children, toys, wood chips, sand and, on this occasion, snow.

Because it was 'wet play', we had some Year 6 children in the class. It was lovely to see them helping the younger ones with their boots, coats, gloves etc. and also helping them with the sledging.

Year 6 children love to be playtime monitors in the Reception class.

The children tried various techniques to build snowmen – rolling, digging with spades, moving handfuls of snow etc. Several snowmen were built during the week.

As mentioned, risk assessments happen constantly. The children had new experiences and faced new challenges. In many schools, the children were not allowed outside because it was considered too dangerous! They missed out on so many learning opportunities.

Dancing

Andreas was very keen to teach everyone some Greek dancing (that he learns at Greek school). He spent over 30 minutes doing this with a large group coming and going, copying his movements and also introducing more movements. Jacqui videoed some of this for the class to watch on the IWB. Two other boys were also dancing to other music later in the day.

This activity demonstrates the level of trust that has built up amongst the children in the class. They understand that no-one is going to laugh at them or ridicule them. Rather, there will be praise and interest in their skill and knowledge. Several practitioners find it difficult to assess whether children respect their own cultures and those of other people. It was clear today that Andreas was proud of his Greek culture and the other children showed respect by wanting to learn the dances too. In a more formal setting, the opportunity for this type of activity would not come about naturally.

Design

Andrew was at the woodwork bench today. I asked him to draw what he was going to make. He drew an aeroplane with two wheels, two engines and a door. He then made the model, adding a ramp for the luggage. He was delighted to see that it compared very well to his design.

This simple intervention moved the activity to a higher level. It would not be appropriate with every child but I knew that Andrew was capable of planning ahead and also of evaluating and adapting his work.

Reference books

Today Lia was making a box, copying the visual instructions in a craft book. She had glued together some lolly sticks (exactly as shown in the book). She had made four pieces exactly the same (for the sides of the box). It was then the end of the day, but she realised that her work would be safe and that she would be able to carry on with it the next day.

Reference books in the creative area give the children ideas for things to make.

A visit to the vet

The guinea pigs both have skin sores, and so on Wednesday I took them to the vets. Fourteen children and one other adult came along too. It was quite a long walk, but very valuable. The staff were very welcoming and keen to educate the group. A nurse showed the children all around the premises, including the operating theatre. The vet used a special low table (he had to kneel down) so that the children could see what was going on. Each guinea pig had an injection. The vet didn't charge us – he said he wanted to encourage schools to have pets and teach children about caring for animals.

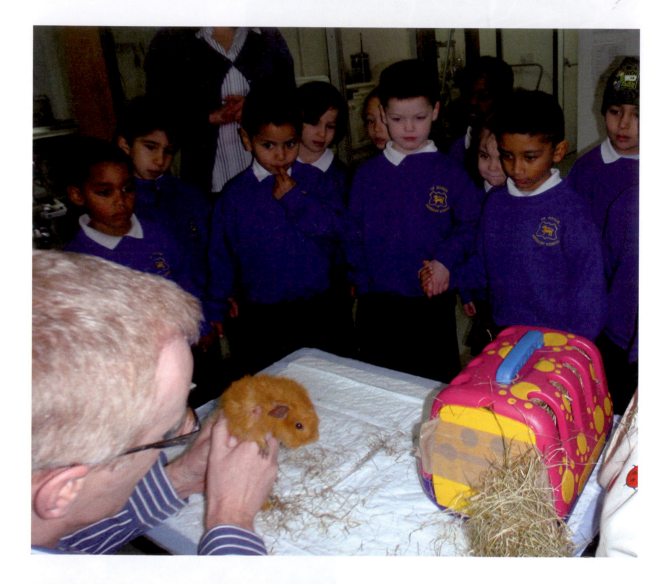

This photo shows the concern on the faces of the children. First-hand experiences such as this are not always easy to organise but the effort is so worthwhile for the children. They talked about this event for days afterwards.

Teddy bears

Further first-hand experiences came about later in the week. Some girls had been making teddy bear robots and Jessica insisted on having a battery for hers, 'otherwise it wouldn't be able to move!'

Battery-powered robot.

Other children then said they wanted to have a 'Teddy Bears' Picnic' and three girls helped Jacqui write a note for the parents. We combined this outing with a trip to see some animals. (This was requested about ten days ago.)

We went to Trent Park and it was very successful, if a little cold. The most exciting thing was feeding the pony. Many children were very scared about this, but one of the ponies was perfectly calm and friendly and gave the children the confidence they needed.

The interaction with live animals led to high levels of involvement in several children who have been difficult to engage.

The new year is off to an exciting start. The children are engaged, enthusiastic and confident. They seek new experiences and pursue their interests with determination – employing adults to help when necessary. No wonder that the spring term sees such huge leaps in development.

In this chapter I will look briefly at the topic of attachment disorder and the role of key workers. With regard to the environment, the role play area indoors and water play outside are described. The examples of activities in the diary section give a clear impression that the children have started to see the value of recording on paper and also of more sophisticated models and games emerging.

FEBRUARY: TO DO LIST

- Update folders.
- Continue second cycle of focus groups.
- Assess phonics.
- Start some children on reading scheme (if appropriate).

Attachment disorder and key workers

Eight years ago, my husband and I became foster carers, and the subject of attachment disorder became a part of our daily lives with the children in our care. In the simplest terms, babies who have their emotional and physical needs met by a caring parent will develop an attachment to that parent. They will then go on to make other attachments and eventually form good relationships as children and adults. The problems arise when a baby's needs are not responded to effectively, consistently or sympathetically. These babies will develop an attachment disorder that can affect them in numerous ways. For example, they may not be able to express needs and emotions in appropriate ways, make friends, trust adults, or relax and become absorbed in activities.

Early Years practitioners should be aware of these possible problems. For some children, their key worker will be the first adult who is going to be consistent and empathetic towards them. In these cases the key worker must build a relationship of trust and empathy with that child. They need to 'hold the child in mind' during and between school sessions. A simple way to demonstrate this to the child is to greet them with a question; for example, 'So how was your shopping trip with Mummy yesterday?' Hopefully, the child will take a small step towards being able to make attachments – a vital life skill. The younger the children, the more important this work is. Therefore, in settings where young babies are cared for, I think the key worker system is crucial – the babies should have just one key worker if at all possible. In a Reception class it is often difficult to establish such a system. There may be only one or two adults for 30 children. Other staff may only work part-time. The key worker tends to be the person who is available at the time, and for most children, by this age, this is effective and adequate.

However, this system is not adequate when dealing with those children who do cause concern. Attachment disorder may be indicated by many things. For example, a child may display low-level involvement, seem unable to make friends, deliberately damage resources or disrupt games, lack emotion or display extreme and inappropriate emotion.

In such cases (whatever the cause), it is vital for that child to have a key person with whom they and their parents can form a trusting relationship.

In our school, this is done on an informal basis when problems and concerns are highlighted. When this happens, we often find that a staff member has already developed a relationship with the child and/or the parent. We then make sure that that person deals with the child and parent whenever possible making extra time for conversations and activities. For us and many other schools this is an area where further staff training and the development of more rigorous procedures are needed.

Setting up the environment

Role play area indoors

Some role play themes recur frequently.

We have a large role play area indoors that is divided into two sections. One is set up as a home corner permanently since the appeal of this and the learning opportunities it offers never seem to wane. In this area we have the following:

- dressing-up clothes (12 items, hung on 12 numbered pegs – a mixture of cloaks, jackets, dresses and tops to appeal to all children)
- mirror
- bags (7 bags, hung on 7 numbered pegs)
- hats (in a box with the number of hats written on the box)

- shoes (in a box with the number of shoes written on the box)
- table
- 4 chairs
- 2 armchairs
- cooker
- dresser
- 4 of each cups, saucers, plates, knives, forks, spoons, eggs, egg cups
- books
- telephone
- notepads, pens and pencils
- 2 dolls
- 2 doll's beds
- unit with drawers containing baby clothes, nappies, bottles etc.
- saucepans and cooking utensils
- small amount of pretend food
- clock
- hairbrushes, clips etc.
- purses and wallets with plastic money.

Everything is set out neatly so that the area is used in a purposeful way and tidied up well too. Occasionally, we add pots of pasta etc. to the home corner but have yet to find a way to make this manageable.

The other section of the role play area is used for various scenarios according to the interests or requests of the children. Over the years we have gathered resources for many options. Each time a new request is made, then this is organised, and once it is dismantled, we keep anything that has been made or found for that particular scene. These resources are kept in large boxes in a storage unit outside the classroom so that they are readily available if the same request is made again. The boxes we have at present include the following, but new ideas may present themselves at any time:

- doctor's surgery
- café
- florist
- dentist
- pizza restaurant
- vet
- under the sea
- travel agent
- shop
- library
- puppet theatre.

We do not make these areas overly elaborate and they do not take long to set up. The children make or add resources as they see the need. In this way, the area can be changed regularly and quickly as soon as interest has faded or as soon as new interests emerge.

Water play outdoors

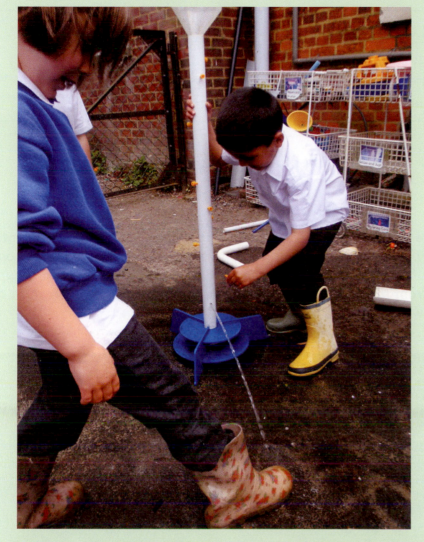

The funky fountain can be seen here with the storage trolleys in the background.

An outside tap (or even a water butt with tap), makes a huge difference to the water-based activities outdoors. The water play resources are stored in the area where they are to be used. The ground is concrete and it is near to the tap. The smaller resources are stored in labelled old art trolleys. The shelving is metal mesh and is ideal, as the rain and water can run through it. The resources in these units include: watering cans, boats, pipes and tubes, water wheels, funnels, jugs, bottles and decorator's brushes, rollers and paint trays. Nearby we have a water tray, a builder's tray on a stand, buckets, a Creative Cascade set, extra guttering, a hose pipe, a funky fountain and wellington boots.

All this equipment is left in place – it is weatherproof and there is no need to put it away. This saves staff having to get equipment out, and means that it is always available to be used. Even in freezing weather this area still attracts children as the water left in the trays turns to ice and opens new avenues of exploration. In very hot weather the water play takes on another new dimension when the children can actually get **in** the water (see the summer months for examples).

Diary extracts: examples of development and learning

WHAT TO LOOK OUT FOR
- Children begin to use phonics to write.
- Children start recording maths in various ways.
- Models are more intricate and carefully designed.

Many of the extracts below give examples of the subjects mentioned in this list.

A show needs tickets

Today a group of girls were singing – using microphones that they had made with cardboard tubes and newspaper. Following a suggestion from an adult, they agreed to put on a show but then decided independently that they needed tickets. They worked as a group and got every name card from the graphics area and wrote the name of each child on a ticket. The show was very well attended.

Copying names onto tickets for the show.

A bird's nest sparks new learning

A group found an old nest outside. They started to make their own nests with grass, twigs etc. This was very difficult and led the children to admire the skill of birds immensely. As a result of this, Jacqui took a group to the school library to find books on nests. Later, some children made eggs with clay. This led to lots of counting and also some addition games.

The clay eggs were used for maths games.

Worry dolls

Whilst in the library, Jacqui found a book from Guatemala about worry dolls. She read this to the class and then a large group made their own worry dolls.

Worry dolls.

The message from the book was that you tell the doll your worry, put it under your pillow and it won't worry you anymore. The children were remarkably willing to discuss their worries and it was enlightening to hear their concerns.

Sustained, complex activity

Jas did some woodwork today, with a definite plan to make a 'cat'. She found two blocks and asked how to join these together. I showed her how to add a strip of wood at the back. She did this, but with the second nail the strip broke. 'Oh that can be the ears!' She then found a new block to form the body. She added a pipe cleaner for a tail and then took the cat indoors to decorate. Once it was complete she insisted on writing a story about the cat. I sat with her and she was able to sound out 'cat' and several other words and was keen to take the pen from me and write any of the words that she felt confident about.

The thin strip of wood is used to join the two large blocks together.

Ready to read?

Jacqui did a phonic assessment on each child using the six sounds – s a t n i p – to see if they could say the correct sound when shown the letter, pick the letter out when the sound was heard, make short words using the letters and read short words made up of those letters. Ten of the 42 children could do this very well and so we have decided to start these ten on the reading scheme. We are also sending home library books for all children, which we ask the parents to read to the children regularly.

The use of the reading scheme is another subject that is discussed and reviewed each year. We see it as a structured tool, which helps many children progress to independent reading within a year. It is a means to an end and used with caution!

Show jumping in class

Today, two girls were playing with a Lego horse. I encouraged them to build some jumps for the horses and then to make numbers to stick on the jumps. Each girl then had a turn jumping the horse over the jumps in the correct order, then shut their eyes while I rearranged the jumps. The challenge was to find each number in turn to jump over. One of the girls made a stand for the spectators and another child joined in and made a 'start' and 'finish' sign.

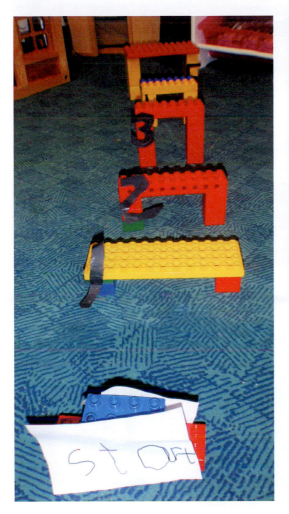

These were two girls who had been identified as needing to work on number recognition. This can now be extended to an outdoor obstacle course with numbers.

The local area

Drawing houses is always popular and today Alison directed this activity into a group activity, forming a road, and then this extended onto three large sheets covering the local area. Lejdina drew items from the park, another child drew the vet's, another child drew the theatre. In each case some writing was encouraged in the form of labels according to the ability of the child.

Several children contributed to this display.

A skeleton came to class

Smile for the camera.

Whenever I am out of the classroom, it is always exciting to return and see what has been happening. Sometimes I look through the pictures on the camera and find photos of events that I have not been aware of at all. The photo above was one such example. The skeleton came and went again. I didn't see it at all. The children continue to explore and learn, whichever adult is in the room – they do not become reliant on their teacher.

Children writing

Several children are now very keen to write. For example, today Jessica insisted on writing a story about Jacqui and was determined to do the writing herself. She needed an adult with her to help with the sounds that she has not yet learnt. However, she was able to sound out all the words independently and if she did not know how to form a letter, she asked the adult to model this for her. She was delighted with the finished piece, and at the end of the day she read it to the class, while Jacqui acted it out!

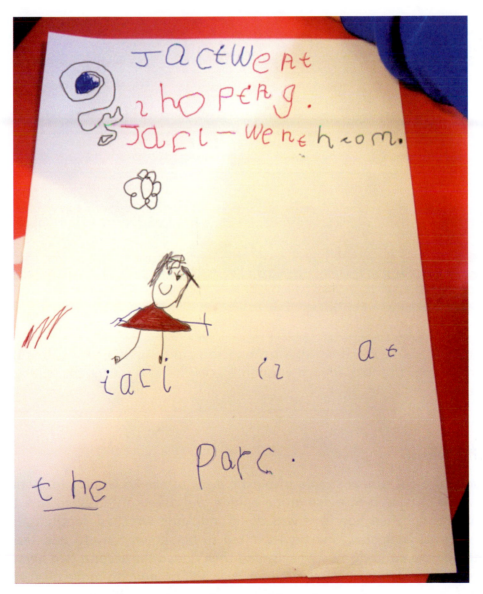

'Jaci went shoping. Jaci went hom. Jaci is at the parc'.

Football

In the playground a group was playing football. It is very funny to watch four-year-olds playing football as they tend to just charge around kicking the ball in any direction. I noticed that there was quite a bit of pushing and so I introduced myself as the referee with yellow and red cards. The children knew what these meant and agreed that there would be two minutes time out for offenders. This helped greatly and eventually I moved away, and the players each took a turn at being the ref.

We use a corner of the infant playground for games such as football and tennis as the garden does not have a large enough space. This also means that the activities in the garden are not disrupted.

New skills learnt

On Thursday we got a new supply of plastic discs to use as wheels (donated by a local factory). Anne was keen to make an aeroplane and asked an adult to saw the wood for her. The adult modelled how this was done and Anne watched carefully, but was very reluctant to touch the saw. She then wanted to be shown how to add the wheels and again watched the adult do two wheels, and then added the second two herself. The adult then moved away and Anne persevered for over half an hour to make a second aeroplane without any help.

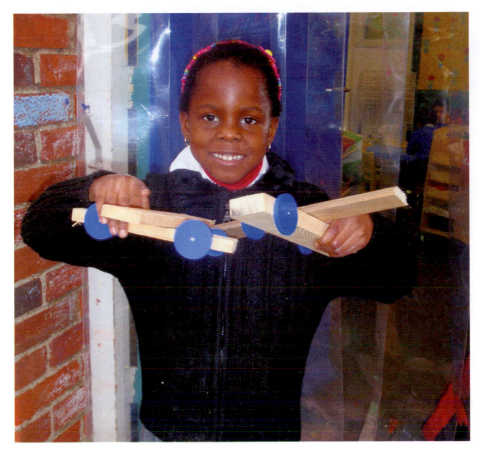

The plastic strips can be seen hanging in the doorway behind Anne. These mean that we can have the door open but the cold air is kept out of the classroom.

Perfume production

A few weeks ago, some of the children planted the seeds from their apples in little flower pots. These have now started to grow. This inspired Jessica to make her own plant in a pot. She then said that it needed perfume to make it smell and since we didn't have any perfume an adult showed her how to use the lavender plant from the garden to crush in water and make perfume. This led to a whole group making perfume by crushing various leaves.

A request is made for 'perfume'.

Perfume is produced!

A vet's surgery

The children have started taking animals into the role play area and using it as a vet's. We therefore decided to create a vet's surgery there.

Pet details

Type of animal: ʃihep Maxeip

Symptoms: blob dolg zod

Treatment: ihJɛch cotonItw

> With each role play area we include writing opportunities if appropriate. The children had seen how much the vet recorded when we took the guinea pigs to see him. In role, they started to write about each animal that visited their surgery.

This month, as in every month, there was no forward planning necessary to ensure that every aspect of the curriculum was covered. The curiosity and enthusiasm of the children, combined with the provision, led to learning in all areas, as the examples above show.

In this chapter, I explain why it is essential to have the support of the senior management team. I also describe some activities that take place during the whole-class carpet sessions. The section about the environment looks at the carpet area indoors, role play outdoors and planting in general. The diary section has numerous examples to show how, in some instances, the adults support the next steps in children's learning. On other occasions, the children support each other and, in many cases, they are confident and ambitious enough to take the next step themselves.

MARCH: TO DO LIST

- Discuss plans with SMT (new budget comes in April).
- Celebrate progress of children in Year 1.
- Complete second cycle of focus groups.

Support from the SMT

The central principle behind the work at our school is a belief that children learn best by pursuing their own interests. Without the support of the senior staff, this becomes very difficult, if not impossible. Support is needed in many ways, as shown in Figure 7.1.

Support from SMT is essential to...

- Provide adequate staffing – to allow free flow indoors and out as well as observation, flexibility and support of children in their activities.
- Allow a different timetable to the rest of the school – with no pressure to attend assemblies, playtimes, lessons outside the classroom etc.
- Fund adequate provision – both indoors and outside.
- Remove pressure for more formal teaching – to allow children to develop as individuals on their own learning journey.
- Advocate for this way of working – to advisers, parents and inspectors.

Figure 7.1 Support from SMT

I have visited settings where the management are undermining the staff in various ways. Some head teachers insist that the Reception teacher hears every child read every day. How can that teacher do anything else? Other head teachers insist on pursuing a phonic scheme that dictates that there has to be one hour of direct teaching of phonics every day. It is no wonder that in those classes the children rarely opt to write during their 'free time'. If there is no budget for setting up the outdoor play area or for ongoing maintenance, then how can there be high-quality outdoor provision? Some head teachers want to see (and, more worryingly, want the children to see) a clear distinction between 'play' and 'work'. This indicates that they do not believe that children **learn through their play** and would not therefore support this way of working. Children **should not see a distinction between play and work.** If they do, they see 'work' as something to be got out of the way so that they can get on with what is valuable to them.

Head teachers are under enormous pressure from parents, advisers and inspectors and the criteria for success are KS2 test results. In our school, it has been impossible to see the long-term effects of our methods because we have such high mobility. In the current Year 6 class there are only five children who were in our Reception class. In the current Year 5 class there are only three. We are fortunate to have a head who believes in the work we are doing and is supported by the Early Years Strategy Manager for the borough.

Although it has not been possible to track many children through the whole school, I often see the children in KS1. This month, in Year 1, the children were writing in their progress books – an assessment activity that is done once each half-term throughout the school. It was wonderful to see the writing these children were producing. In particular, the EAL children, who were just starting to talk freely at the end of Reception, were producing whole pages of writing and they were delighted to do it.

Year 1 – independent writing in March.

This dramatic progress, combined with the enthusiasm and confidence shown by the children, helps to persuade the Head Teacher that we are doing the right thing by these children.

Carpet sessions

I have already described some of the main uses of the whole–class carpet sessions: story acting (see Chapter 4), phonic lessons (Chapter 5), showing photos from families (Chapter 2). In addition, the sessions may be used for singing, story time, poems, rhymes, watching films, showing children's 'work', modelling the use of new equipment or a new game, or discussions. We have gathered a selection of props for favourite poems, rhymes and songs, which are stored in fabric wallets near the carpet, along with cards with the text on them. In this way, the children can revisit these at any time and they also help new staff in the class.

Setting up the environment

The carpet area indoors

One self-serve storage unit can be seen at the back of this photo. These are ideal for the classroom and relatively inexpensive.

We have made the carpet area as large as possible and it is nearly always occupied and being used productively. Around the edge of the carpet are numerous 'self–service' storage units. The interactive whiteboard is at one edge of the carpet so that it can be used for whole-class sessions and is still accessible for the children to use independently at other times.

One of the most valuable resources is the set of community blocks. These are set out on a bookshelf with silhouettes of the blocks so that the children can tidy them away efficiently. Our nursery nurse spent several hours preparing this system, but it will last for years.

The shadowing for the block storage can be seen on the shelving behind this model.

Other resources include:

- construction toys (Lego, Duplo, Knex, Brio construction, etc.)
- wooden train set
- floor puzzles
- farm and animals etc.
- sets of various animals, dinosaurs etc.
- toy cars
- dolls' house and accessories
- Playmobil sets
- puppets and puppet theatre
- shapes (2D and 3D)
- mini-blocks in a basket
- nesting dolls.

This is not a definitive list; the main aim should be to have a wide selection of open-ended, flexible, good-quality resources that will appeal to as many different interests as possible.

Role play outdoors

Cakes for the journey.

The role play outdoors can be spread over a wide area, can be a lot more lively and can be far more messy than indoors. Therefore, superhero play, cooking with sand and travelling the world usually take place outside! As with indoors, we try to have as many resources available at all times and stored nearby. The only items that we put away and have to get out each morning are the dolls' buggies and the rail of dressing-up clothes. The large wooden blocks are always available (unless it is raining – see Chapter 3). We also have a large box with hats and bags, a salt bin with fabric and another with dolls and accessories. As explained in Chapter 2, the sand play area has cooking equipment and, of course, the caravan (see Chapter 3) is a delightful place to play.

It is more difficult to set up areas that will last for long periods outdoors, but the children seem to accept this. They often set up a café, doctor's or mechanic's for the day and understand that it needs to be packed away from the elements and the animals overnight.

Planting

These old sinks had been removed from a washroom, but became lovely planters.

Children can read books or watch TV programmes about plants and how to look after them. However, as with all learning for young children, they only develop an understanding of plants and their needs by growing some themselves. This can be achieved indoors or outside quite easily – beans will grow almost anywhere. However, with an enthusiastic adult, fruit, vegetables and flowers of all sorts can be cultivated outside. We started off by just digging over a small area of grass and using this for vegetables. We then got some tubs for herbs, and this year Jacqui has used some of the old sinks and filled them with flowers. The initial work is time-consuming but the children love to help, the discussions are complex and the levels of involvement are high. Equipment needed is minimal – spades, forks and watering cans. The challenge is to get started and then to maintain the areas throughout the year.

Diary extracts: examples of development and learning

![magnifying glass] **WHAT TO LOOK OUT FOR:**
- More children reading independently.
- Children supporting each other.
- Children extending their own learning.

These extracts demonstrate the various sources of stimulus and support that are available to the children. The message is clear – the teacher is just one of many possible sources.

Resources can stimulate and adults support

Lia continues to display amazing design and cutting skills. On this piece she has written a caption at the top of the picture – 'shep 2 in a fd' (sheep – 2 in a field).

The wobbly eyes were the initial stimulus for this picture. An adult approached and Lia requested help to write at the top of the picture. The adult brought over the phonic card and encouraged Lia to say the sounds of the words. The adult pointed out the sounds that Lia did not know.

Peer group support

Alice wanted Isabel to join her game and said, 'Come on Isabel, dance and I will play the music'. Isabel replied, 'I'm a bit embarrassed'. Alice then said, 'Don't be embarrassed, we won't look!'

In this example, one child is supporting another to help her have the courage to dance! The musical instruments are available every day and are used regularly.

Willing to try

Dahir was watching a group skip with a long rope. He then started writing their names down on labels and recording how many skips they did. When I had a turn, he wrote, 'Ana 32'. He stayed at this activity for over 20 minutes.

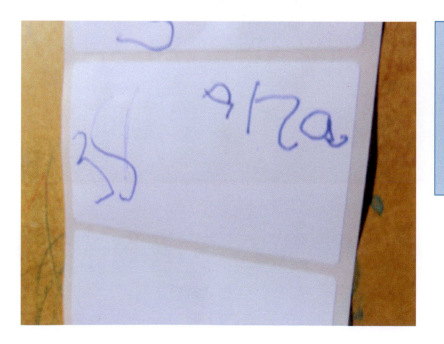

The availability of clipboards, labels and pens provided the support that this child needed in order to take the next step – recording names and scores.

0800 310 0781

FREE on

Request more information on Northwich **TODAY**. Simply complete the form below, call us on **0800 310 0781** or visit **www.mccarthyandstone.co.uk**

You may be contacted via the methods of communication for which you have provided details. Where a mobile number has been provided, you may also be contacted by SMS or other electronic means.

Please send me my free colour brochure

Please tick all that apply.

Interest: For myself ☐   Friend/Relative ☐

New properties ☐   Pre-owned ☐

For news and information from the **McCarthy & Stone Group** post to: Freepost RSBL-TXHJ-TBAY, McCarthy & Stone Retirement Lifestyles Ltd., BOURNEMOUTH BH8 8EZ

^Charges may apply for mobile phone users.

Title	Name

Address

Postcode	Tel

Email

McCarthy & Stone

Later Life. Greater Life

Beautiful one and two bedroom
Assisted Living retirement
apartments for the over 70s
coming soon

McCarthy & Stone

Later Life. Greater Life

Retirement living coming soon to Northwich

Our new purpose-built development for the over 70s will consist of 58 one and two bedroom Assisted Living apartments. Now is the time to find out how our new development, coming soon to Chester Way, Northwich can help you enjoy a greater, later life.

Register now to express your interest

www.mccarthyandstone.co.uk

Support from numerous sources

These pictures show Safia's work developing at the woodwork bench – from an initial 2D idea to a 3D model.

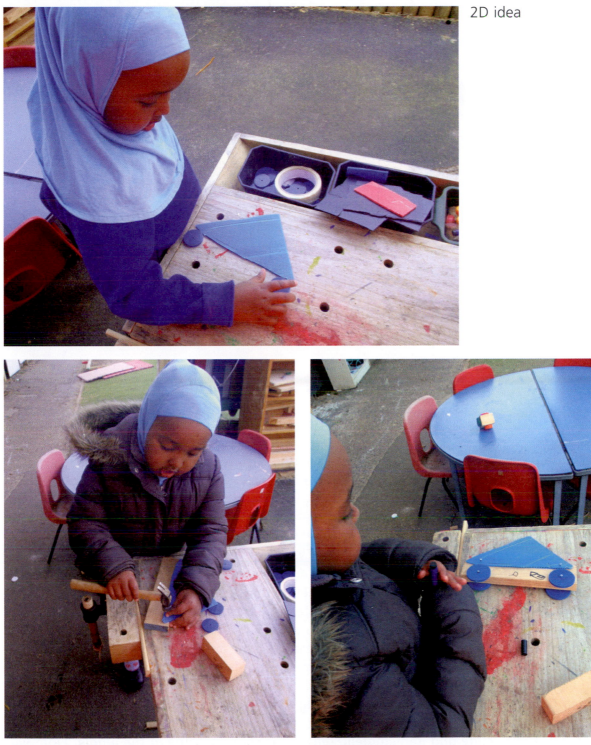

2D idea

The idea develops

3D model

In this example, Safia had observed other children at the woodwork bench and this gave her ideas, she then asked an adult to help her with the initial hammering of the nails and finally decided to draw on windows herself. Many next steps were taken with support from different sources.

Supporting writing

Some children were making cards for Mother's Day and Liam approached me saying, 'I want to write "I love my mum".' I sat with him and supported him in this. When he had finished he said, 'I want to write it again!' I gave him another piece of paper and he copied the phrase again. He then said, 'I want to write it again' and he copied the phrase for a third time! Several other boys had seen what was going on and they joined in with the activity.

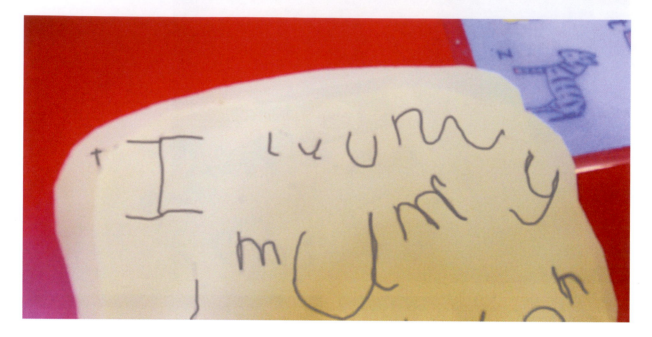

> As stated before, the children are never told to write; they often ask to write, and it is at that point that the adult intervention can be most productive.

By the end of the day, we had about 20 messages inside the cards – all initiated by the children and supported by the staff. While I was helping these children, I observed Dean and Serif together. Each had a piece of paper and a pencil and they had collected an alphabet card from the graphics area. They sat together and started saying, 'Right – "The Power Rangers came" – OK p p...'. They each wrote a 'p' on the page. I was called away and when I returned they had written 'pw r...' and were saying 'j – what's j? j j j for...' I said, 'j for jug'. They then found the jug and wrote a 'j' on the page. They continued writing the string of letters for their story and persevered for about 30 minutes with this. Eventually, they had four lines of writing and announced, 'We have written our own story!' They then pegged the papers in the graphics area, ready to be read to the class and acted out later.

They then ran outside and immediately joined in a chasing game in the jungle. Liam was involved in the game too.

The purpose and learning involved in this game are harder to define – physical development and spatial awareness, social skills in negotiating, understanding how far the excitement can build, role play and language development. The contrast in the appearance and outcomes of the two activities could not have been greater and yet the levels of involvement and enjoyment were equal. That cannot often be said of boys' writing in a Reception class, compared to their chasing games!

Collaboration in a new venture

Anne and Lia have become friendly this week. Today they were at the woodwork bench for over 30 minutes and created this colourful piece combining 2D and 3D. They nailed on pieces of corroflute and added felt-pen drawings as well.

There was no adult involvement in this activity and yet it was a novel and ambitious piece of work. The two girls supported each other in this new venture.

More writing

Lia and Anne were making books today. Anne said, 'I want to write "To grandma from Anne"'. I sat with her to write the message – she knew most of the sounds. She was able to sound out 'granma' and 'from'. She went on to add pictures on each page and label them using sounds. At one point I saw her write 'crisms' for 'Christmas', independently. At the same time, Tanyel was working at another table and was labelling a picture. She is just beginning to enjoy using sounds to write independently. She only came to get an adult to help with the 'v' sound – amazing!

Tanyel wanted to label her picture and an adult was available to give her encouragement. She didn't need help with the task; rather, a reassuring presence.

Organised chaos

I saw a group of boys playing in the jungle area today. At a glance it looked like chaotic charging around with buggies. When I asked them what the game involved, they explained that they were all 'nannies', that each nanny had to have a handbag, in which was a carefully selected book. During the game, they had to go into the jungle, find an animal and use two books from separate bags as a trap for catching the animals. What had appeared as chaos was, indeed, far from it.

St Patrick's Day

On St Patrick's Day, Tina was wearing a green ribbon. When the children asked her why, she said it was because she was Irish. Jessica then said, 'Oh we do Irish dancing' (remembering being taught by Lorna earlier in the year). We then put on the CD and a whole group started to do Irish dance steps in the garden.

> This next step – linking a green ribbon, with the Irish culture of another child and then linking this to a particular style of dancing – came about because the children are confident enough to have conversations and ask questions.

A photo of a café

Christina's pictures from home showed a trip to a café. Several children liked the look of this and so we went in two groups to the local café.

Several children 'read' the newspapers in the café.

Back at school we changed the role play area to a café and the children immediately fell into the roles of customers or staff. Some children took the work very seriously, using all their phonics skills to write the orders and then bringing the correct food to the table.

First-hand experiences are some of the best ways to stimulate children, and this was clearly evident after the trip to the café.

Confident children extend their own learning

The enthusiasm for woodwork continues. The children are combining different materials and resources from different areas to achieve the result they want. Alice produced a dog and then decided it needed to have a skateboard. The two were joined together with an elastic band.

Praise and encouragement were all that were needed for this child to take her work to the next level. She has already developed the woodworking skills and, with time to think, she came up with the idea of using the elastic band to secure her dog onto its skateboard!

It is clear from these examples that the children view the adults as one of many possible sources of ideas and support. It is one of the most important outcomes of this way of working. The children want to learn and will make use of everything, and everyone, around them.

8 April

The Easter holiday in 2010 took up the first two weeks of April. Also in that month, a volcano erupted in Iceland sending an ash cloud into the skies over Europe. All flights were suspended, which meant that I, along with thousands of others, was unable to return to the UK for a further week. Thus my time in school in April was very short indeed. In the first section of this chapter, I will look at building a partnership with parents and also briefly discuss 'wet play'. In the environment section I will look at ICT and music provision. There are just a few activities described in the diary section. These reflect the start of spring, the response to the volcanic events and the further development of writing.

APRIL: TO DO LIST

- Settle children back into routines after the holiday.
- Begin final cycle of focus groups.
- Assess phonic progress and split into groups if necessary.
- Negotiate budget for Early Years.

Partnership with parents

It is essential to work in partnership with parents if the children are to achieve their full potential. Conversely, if parents, for whatever reason, are in disagreement with the school, this affects the children in a negative way. At De Bohun, we are still working to improve this aspect of our work. I have already described some of the ways in which we try to build these partnerships:

- Transition work (e.g. parents attend stay-and-play sessions)
- Home visits
- Family photos displayed in class
- Parents help during induction period
- Consultation sheets for focus children
- Digital cameras to get photographs from home
- Noticeboard for parents to consult
- Termly parents' meetings
- Parents contribute to folders
- Staff available for discussions each day
- Parents welcome in class whenever they wish
- Weekly 'planning' sheets displayed on noticeboard
- Information leaflets sent home
- Activities to do at home

Figure 8.1 Building partnerships with parents

In addition to these things, the school sends out regular newsletters and we also invite parents to information meetings when we feel particular issues need discussing.

However, each year we have one or two parents who are unhappy with us for various reasons. Each time a parent raises a new problem, we discuss possible solutions and explain ideas to parents, and hopefully improve the relationship. Once parents see that their child is happy and making good progress, they are usually reassured, the partnership is restored and a positive cycle is re-established.

Ideas for future development of these partnerships include the following: enabling parents to access their child's Learning Journeys via the internet; producing a high-quality information leaflet to give to parents at the home visit; regular information meetings for parents (various topics); and encouraging parents to tell the school about family events on a regular basis, rather than just when their child is a focus child.

Some of these ideas, and others, will be put into practice in the coming months. This is another area where we constantly review, reflect and amend our practice.

Wet play

Wet play often causes staffing issues in schools. When it is raining the children are not able to access the infant playground. On such occasions, I usually opt to spend the lunch hour in the class with the children. This means that they can still use the garden and class-room. I am very reluctant to swap to the school wet play system, which sees one dinner lady with the whole class indoors, using boxes of 'wet play' toys. The behaviour usually deteriorates and the children have to learn a whole new set of expectations and rules. This seems very unfair. It also leaves us with a class of agitated and sometimes upset children as well as a room in an awful mess! This is no-one's fault; it is just that the staffing does not allow for proper supervision at wet lunchtimes when all the infants are split into their rooms. In the Reception area, we have several spare raincoats, umbrellas and wellington boots. The weather rarely stops us using the garden. We also have a small sheltered area with the woodwork bench and painting area, and the roof above the sand pit keeps off most of the rain. If I stay with the children at lunchtime, it means that the mealtime supervisor can watch some children indoors and I can allow others to be outside.

Fun in the rain.

Setting up the environment

ICT

We impose limits and boundaries on the use of computers.

As mentioned, we have an interactive whiteboard in the classroom. This can be used for whole-class or group teaching, using CD-ROMs and showing DVDs and photos. It is always turned on and children access it independently for games, drawing, writing etc. It is very popular for maths games involving number recognition, ordering, addition and subtraction, as well as games about shapes. We also have two PCs in the classroom and the children use these independently as well. As with any resource, the adults will model the use of the equipment when necessary and will show children how to access particular games or programmes.

The PCs are the only equipment in the Reception class where we have found it necessary to restrict the time spent here by children. This is an issue for most schools, with children waiting near the computer for a turn and also not being willing to get off the computer once they sit down. I have also had several parents complaining that they cannot get their child off the computer games at home. The addictive nature of some games is concerning but, at least in school, we are able to establish boundaries and limits. We use a sand timer to indicate the amount of time each child can spend on the computer. We also have a list of names by the computer and the children cross their name off when they have had a turn. They cannot then have another turn until all the children in the class have had a turn (if they wish). At that point a new list is put up and the cycle starts again.

Diary: Alex has been helping children to access the Ben 10 games. The other children call him over to access the games for them. When we watched him, he was using Google to search for 'araba O . . .' which is a Turkish website, through which he can get to the Ben 10 games. We have now written the word 'araba 0' on a piece of paper near the computer so that the other children can access this themselves!

Other ICT equipment we use on a regular basis includes the following: digital cameras (the children use these themselves at home and school), video camera, printers, tape recorder, CD player, light box, metal detectors, shop tills, mobile phones, photocopiers, beep bots and other remote-controlled toys.

We have bought very robust cameras so that the children can use them independently.

Music

Music, in one form or another, occurs daily in our class. Songs and rhymes are enjoyed both indoors and outside, accompanied by the guitar, a CD or a computer program. We often use Makaton to sign with the songs. This is a great way to encourage the use of language for all children. CDs are used indoors and outside for dance too. The children make instruments, both indoors in the creative area and outside, mainly at the woodwork bench. We have a large selection of instruments, which we store in the garage and bring out on most days.

Diary extracts: examples of development and learning

The following extracts show that, although the children were only in school for two weeks in April, there were exciting events and great enthusiasm for writing.

A visit to the florist

Tina was animated, talking about her mum's friend who runs a flower shop. On Tuesday a group of ten children went by bus to visit the shop. On the way back to school, the group collected petals and blossom. Once in the classroom, these were used for collage creations. Tina also wanted to press some flowers (having seen this in one of the craft books). We couldn't find a press, but improvised with some wood and vices. The visit also led to several children making paper flowers and so the role play area was transformed into a florist's.

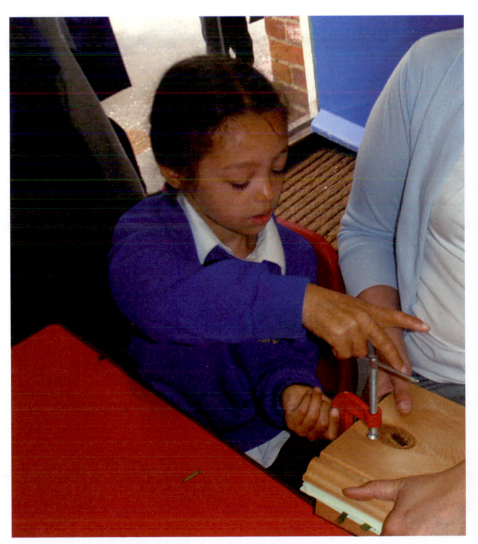

A flower press is created.

Some of the resources produced for the florist will be kept for future use.

Volcanoes

Because I was not back in class, the children started to ask questions about where I was and why I could not get back to school. This led to a great deal of discussion about volcanoes, and information books were found for the children to look at. One adult then found a model volcano in the science resource cupboard, and with some vinegar and bicarbonate of soda they were able to model an eruption. The children were fascinated and used the information books to compare the pictures to the model.

A world event led to discussions and activity in the classroom.

Phonics continues

The phonics programme is continuing and nearly all initial sounds have now been covered. Six children are not coping with these sessions and still need phase 1 work. They are now being taken to another room during these short sessions for rhyming games, playing 'I Spy' etc. The other children are coping well and are retaining the information. For example, Kubir was able to write several words including 'bad', 'got' and 'end', while dictating a story to me. He was also able to make plausible suggestions when sounding out quite complex words.

The children are proud of their ability to make and read short words and keen to show off these skills. They understand how useful these sounds can be when it comes to the important work of writing their stories, shopping lists and letters. For example, Tanyel has overcome her concerns about errors and is now writing several sentences independently, as seen below:

my mum lovs to do the gardenimg her dress gets messy shi planted a red rose an it is looks bootithol. (My Mum loves to do the gardening. Her dress gets messy. She planted a red rose and it (is) looks beautiful.)

Posting letters

A group of girls started playing pirates, which led to hidden treasure and treasure maps. Books about pirates were found, and once the maps were drawn the girls wanted to know where would be safe to hide them. Eventually it was decided to put them in envelopes and post them to their houses. This led to discussions about addresses and the postal system. Several other children then wanted to write letters to post and this became the main activity of the afternoon, with some fantastic results. Kubir, Dahir and Andreas were particularly attracted to this idea. One of their letters is shown below.

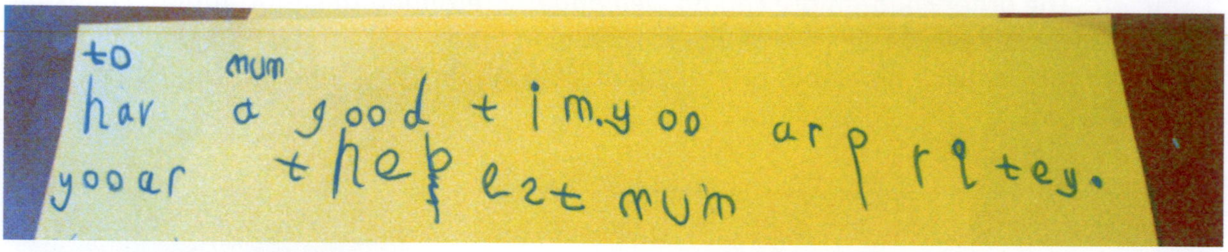

'to mum
Hav a good tim.
Yoo ar pritey
Yoo ar the best mum'

Elena also wrote a letter to her new baby sister. Help was given with the letters needed to make the sounds 'ar' and 'ng' and to spell the word 'like'; but otherwise, Elena wrote this independently. Eventually, 13 children had written letters and they all walked up to the post box to send them off.

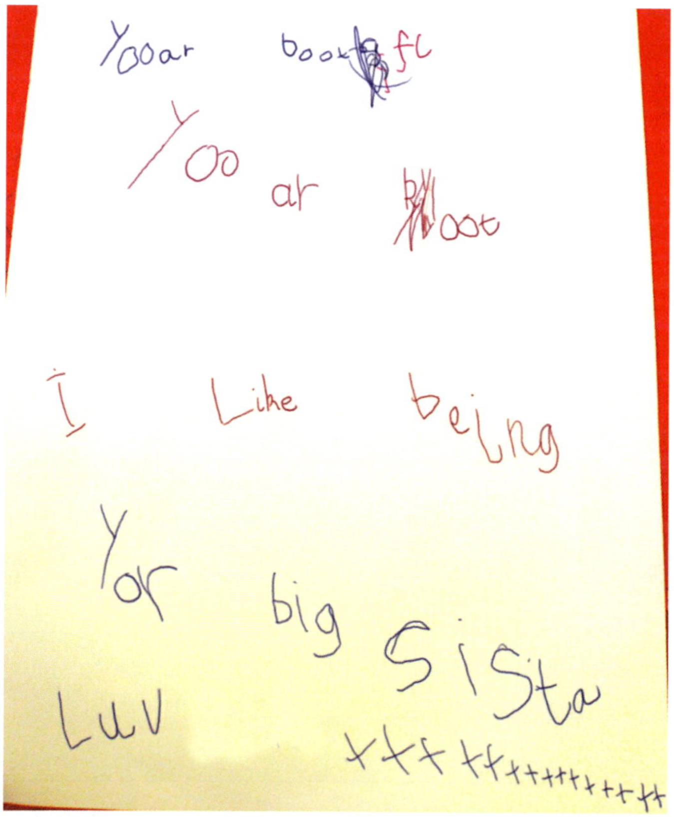

'Yoo ar bootfl
Yoo ar kyoot
I Like being yor big sista'

(bootfl = beautiful, kyoot = cute)

During the final few months of the academic year, the children often make sudden leaps in their development. In April this year, these leaps were most evident in the children's writing. Without any pressure to do so, they were all keen to use these new skills as often as possible. A wonderful start to the final term.

9   May

Each year, during the month of May, we get information about the children who will be joining us for the next academic year. Meanwhile, the current year group are making dramatic progress in all areas. This chapter reflects aspects of both these subjects. In the environment section, I will describe the play dough and cooking area indoors and some aspects of exploration and investigation, both indoors and out. The diary this month reflects the creative themes that were prevalent in the class.

MAY: TO DO LIST

- Begin final cycle of parent meetings.
- Write reports for focus children each week.
- Continue 1–1 ten-minute sessions with each child once per week.
- Send out invitations to 'Stay and Play' sessions for new intake of children.
- Make appointments and visit new children in their preschools.
- Arrange dates for nursery children to start coming for play sessions.
- Agree particular times when prospective families can visit the class.
- Enjoy the warm weather!

Preparations for the new intake

Administration becomes a key task in May. We have the names of the children who have accepted places for September. We also have many prospective parents requesting appointments to see the school, and if they accept a place they are added to the list. One task is to start making appointments to **visit children in their preschool settings** (if they are not in our nursery). This needs to be started as soon as possible since it is usually done during PPA time, and therefore there is only half a day per week for such visits. We also organise some dates for these children to come for **play sessions** and we send out letters inviting them to come along. We no longer organise a meeting for new parents. We found that only about half attended and many could not understand what was being said. We therefore use the home visit to give all the vital information (see Chapter 1). Further arrangements for the new children continue in June.

Assess and review

In the summer term, with the final cycle of focus groups, we prepare a written report for each child too. We share this with the parents at the review meeting during the week following their child's focus week. The report is very short, summarising progress in PSHE, CLL, PSN and other areas. The individual folders give a far more detailed and accurate picture of the learning journeys. The report has a space for the parent to give a comment and they receive a copy of the report to keep. It is quite difficult to choose the focus children early in this final term, since it still seems like a long way to the end of term. However, we stress to the parents that the report reflects their progress to date and that further updates will be added to each folder during the rest of the term.

Setting up the environment

Play dough and cooking area indoors

Wonderful conversations occur around this table.

In the classroom, we have a table that has two uses – for play dough and for cooking. The play dough and equipment is available all the time from a 'self-service' unit nearby. The accessories are in labelled boxes and include: rolling pins of various styles, cutters, moulds, plastic plates and cutlery, scissors, cooking utensils, small toy cooker and extruders.

If a group are cooking, then the play dough cannot be used as we do not have enough space. We have debated whether the cooking ingredients and equipment should be freely available, too, but we have not found a satisfactory way to manage this yet. Each time we have tried it, the ingredients run out within days. The cooking equipment is kept in another unit nearby, but one which is covered by a piece of fabric. The children know that they can only use this equipment when the fabric has been removed. Equipment includes: ingredients in labelled boxes, bowls, spoons, balances, various baking trays, cutters, knives, cookery books, etc. The new silicone baking trays are fantastic – so many different shapes and sizes and all reuseable. The

Yum!

eggs and margarine are kept in the classroom fridge. We also have a set of aprons specifically for cooking.

Exploring – indoors and outdoors

Curiosity leads to exploration.

Some aspects of exploration have been covered in other sections – ICT equipment, sand, water etc. Apart from these things, Jacqui has set up a shelving unit in the garden on which we can store other equipment needed for exploring and investigating:

- spades and forks
- magnifying glasses
- bug boxes
- binoculars
- magnets
- metal detectors
- reference books.

We also have a box (kept in the garage) with equipment for wind exploration. This contains ribbons, windmills, bubbles, kites etc. There are also two globes kept indoors near the book area, along with numerous non-fiction reference books.

The children can use this equipment indoors, if appropriate. We have one area in the garden that is for digging. It has a wooden post in the middle with laminated pictures of minibeasts as an immediate point of reference for any interesting discoveries.

Exploration leads to discoveries.

A small point to mention, but one which could save you hours of time, is when **laminating for use outdoors**, make sure the laminating sheet is bigger than the picture by at least 2 cm all round. Then, when you staple it to a fence or shelf, make sure the staples do not go through the paper or card, just through the clear laminated sheet. This stops the rain seeping in, and the pictures will then last up to three years.

We also have our 'jungle' area, which is, in fact, just a hill (covering an old air-raid shelter) covered in bushes and trees. The children love to journey deep into this jungle looking for snakes and crocodiles. This is another area of our set-up that causes worried faces from visiting teachers because the children are out of sight, hidden by the bushes. It is in situations like this that self-discipline is so vital. The children have learnt that they need to be responsible for their own actions. If one child is being upset by another, they have learnt to speak to each other, but if the issue is unresolved, they seek out an adult to help. Although adults often venture into the jungle, we are rarely called to sort out disputes, the exception being when new children join the class and need training in these negotiation skills.

One other area of interest is a tiny pond that we have created in an old Butler sink. It is amazing what the children spot in here!

An old sink makes a good pond.

Diary extracts: examples of development and learning

WHAT TO LOOK OUT FOR

- Dramatic progress evident in reading and writing in many children.
- Parents very happy with progress their children are making.
- Children continue to be independent, confident and creative.

The extracts below give a sense of the complete confidence that the children have now gained. As a result of this, they are willing to take risks in terms of creativity and in attempts at new activities.

Perform on stage

The weather is lovely and several times during the week, all but four of the children were outside. Alison helped the children set up a stage using the wooden blocks, cot sides and some fabric. Several children were keen to perform. Some who were hesitant were helped by their friends.

Children gain confidence performing for their friends.

Keep trying

The children are becoming much more confident on the single bar. Most can now lift their legs up and through their arms. Several can roll over the top of the bar. Two more children learnt to ride the two-wheeler bikes this week!

We do not go out of the Reception area for PE lessons – there is no need!

Guitars

Tanyel made a guitar at the wood-work bench and then joined me to play her guitar while the children sang. Several more children have been making guitars. Four girls formed a band and performed outside, and Alex was thrilled with his guitar having spent a long time making it.

Note the children at the snack table in the background of this photo.

Reading and writing

On Tuesday each week we ensure that each child gets some 1–1 time to do phonics, reading and number work (about ten minutes per child). This means that one adult is occupied with this for most of the day, but it is restricted to one day per week. This gives individual children the literacy skills they need in order to complete reading and writing that is necessary for activities that they choose to do.

Two groups made cakes this week and in each case the children were able to read the instructions themselves and carry out all the steps of the process.

See Appendix A for a copy of this cookery book.

Diloo is gaining confidence with her writing each day now. She mentioned that her Grandad has a farm. I asked if she had any photos of the farm. She said she didn't. After further discussion, I took a photo of Diloo with two friends and we printed this. She stuck it on a paper and then wrote a letter to her Grandad in Cyprus (which we have posted to him).

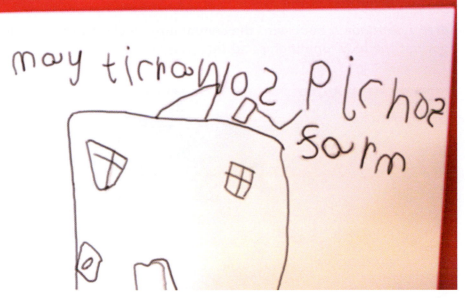

This section of the letter says, 'My teacher wants a picture of the farm'.

The boys' writing is continuing to develop. I watched two boys today who had made a rocket and wanted to write about it. They sat, and each wrote their names and started to sound out the word 'rocket' together. They didn't ask for any help, even though I was at the same table. They were confident in their own ability to do this. Eventually, they had written 'rokit fliy up skiy'. They then pegged this up with the other stories to be read to the class later in the day.

These boys *need* to write in order to get their story on to paper. Then they can read it to the class. That is the motivation for the task.

A boat theme develops

Some children had made a boat with the community blocks and were using the paddles as well. I got out the blow-up dinghy and this caused great excitement.

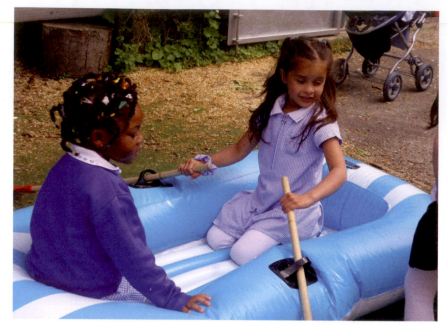

The dinghy was very cheap, but included two oars. I bought it even though I knew the boat would burst in a few days. The oars will last for years.

Andrew said, 'We could put that in the sea and have a ride in it!' A discussion about a trip to the beach ensued and three boys then wrote letters to Mr Scott to ask if we could go to the beach. Eventually, the reply came back saying 'yes!' We then discussed how we would get to the beach. Suggestions included taxis, ambulances and a coach. I then took a group to the office and Andrew spoke to the coach company. We discovered that it would cost £567! The coach is booked for 14 June. Discussions now revolve around how to get this huge amount of money. We had one very hot day and used the opportunity to build a paddling pool with a tarpaulin. This has made the prospect of the beach even more exciting.

The ground under the tarpaulin is tarmac. We raised the edges of the sheet on to milk crates and, in parts, on to the low wall at the back. This makes a massive paddling pool, which can accommodate about 20 children.

Sean came to school

The children know that I have a horse (Sean) and they have been nagging me to bring him to school. At last I managed to organise a day to ride the horse to school. The children were in awe, but fascinated and delighted. When I looked at the photos afterwards, I saw just how huge he must have seemed to such little children. In spite of this, they each came out to pat the horse.

First-hand experiences are memorable and the trigger for wonderful conversations, drawings and imaginative play. I saw a saddle like this during a trip to Melbourne and bought one second-hand. Such a simple idea that leads to so much role play.

The confidence seen this month indicates that the children feel that they can achieve anything. This is exactly how four- and five-year-olds *should* feel. In some settings there are already children being labelled as failures at this age. I was visiting another school recently and heard a four-year-old say, 'Oh, I'm no good at writing'. Children must leave Reception with enthusiasm and excitement about school – something we are very proud to achieve at De Bohun.

10 June

In June we start working with the children who will be coming into Reception in September. We also finalise some assessments on the current class and start to think about the provision they will need for Year 1. However, as you will see in the diary section, the current class continue to develop and have a wonderful month. When reading through these events, it is interesting to note the **mathematical aspect** that is evident in many of them. In the environment section, I will briefly describe water play indoors and art activities outdoors (although much of this has already been covered).

JUNE: TO DO LIST

- Send out appointment letters for home visits in September.
- Arrange times for groups of children from the nursery to come and play.
- Accommodate new children at 'Stay and Play' sessions and talk to the parents.
- Visit new children in their preschools.
- Visit the nursery to see the children there.
- Finalise assessments.
- Update folders.
- Continue writing reports for focus children.

Transition work in June

New Reception children

Children who have accepted places at our school are keen to get as much information as possible. At this time, we send them a letter with an **appointment for a home visit** in September.

Children from our school nursery come over to visit in small groups and stay for an hour at a time. This means that they will be familiar with the room, garden and some staff before they start in September.

We also have hour-long **'Stay and Play' sessions for children who are not in our nursery.** They are invited to two sessions, in groups of about five. We also try to **visit these children in their preschools.** Although this is difficult to organise, it is very valuable. It is a chance to see the children in a setting where they are confident and relaxed and to speak to staff at the preschool about the child. In addition, we **visit our own nursery** to see these children in their familiar environment too. (Obviously, this is easier to organise.)

Assessments of current Reception class

The Foundation Stage Profile data has to be finalised for the end of June. This is also the month when most school-based **assessments are completed** and the information passed on to the senior managers and the Year 1 staff. The **individual folders** are the most important aspect of this work and these are all **updated** during this month. Further transition work and assessments will continue into July.

Setting up the environment

Water play indoors

Numerous mathematical and scientific concepts are grasped during water play.

As with sand play, there is a contrast between outdoors and indoors. Water play indoors needs to be contained within a water tray (although the floor will, of course, get wet). Thus the equipment available is smaller than the outdoor resources, but no less varied and interesting. As usual, it is stored in containers with clear labels and is accessible at all times. The resources include the following, but there are many more possibilities:

- jugs and bottles
- measuring containers (various shapes and sizes)
- syringes
- plastic water creatures
- shells and stones
- water wheels
- funnels
- sieves

- ladles and other utensils
- aprons hung up nearby.

The water tray is placed near to the sinks for filling and emptying. There is a mop nearby, which the children can use to clean up any spillages. We also add things to the water on various occasions – food colouring, glitter, washing-up liquid, soap flakes.

As with all areas, the children know that they can bring other resources to the water tray, such as toy people and boats they have made. Equally, they are able to make decisions about what is not acceptable to bring – such as play dough.

Art outdoors

Art work occurs in some of the outdoor areas that have already been described. For example, craft activities often occur outside using resources from the graphics shelves. The woodwork involves design and the models are often then decorated. There is drawing on the chalk board and whiteboard as well as painting with water on the ground and walls etc. There are also pens, pencils and paper in the caravan, and several children like to sit in there to draw. In addition to these things, we always have large paper and paints available outdoors, and often two children will paint a picture together.

The outdoor easel is large enough to allow children to work in pairs if they wish.

Occasionally we use gloss paint on pieces of marine plywood, as this produces artwork that can be left outdoors and displayed on the walls in the garden and play-ground. This is a very messy activity, but well worth it for the long-term results.

Diary extracts: examples of development and learning

WHAT TO LOOK OUT FOR

- New children enjoy their play sessions in the Reception class.
- Assessments show good progress in all areas for most children.
- Mathematical awareness increases.

Activities this month covered all aspects of the curriculum, but it is interesting to note that there was a mathematical focus to many of the activities.

Cultural awareness

Isabel and Jenna spent over 30 minutes building this house (with integral bus!). They then started to make numbers to stick on to the seats and got up to number 12. I joined their game and asked where the bus was going. 'Turkey!' said Isabel. (She has relatives in Turkey.) I asked her where Jenna wanted the bus to go and she said 'Poland!' (Jenna is Polish.) She then went on to name several children in the class and where they would want the bus to go, e.g. Andreas: 'Cyprus', Anne: 'Nigeria'. I was amazed at how much knowledge the children had gained about each other.

This block play led to discussions about various countries and links to children in the class.

Later in the morning, Isabel built another bus outside. I was again intrigued to see that she knew which number-plate went at the front. 'It's the white one, I've seen it on my car.'

Small models built indoors are often replicated on a larger scale outdoors.

Number hunt

In the garden, the children had been 'searching' for various creatures, children and foxes. Jacqui decided to latch on to this enthusiasm and hid the numbers 1–20 in the jungle area without saying anything to the children. Some children soon spotted a few numbers and then a large group joined the search. Isabel decided she needed a way of keeping track of the numbers she had found, and created a grid on which she could tick them off as they were spotted. She said, 'a thirteen is a 3 and a 1' and she wrote '31'. This reversal was pointed out to her and the later numbers were written correctly. She then took her grid out to the jungle and spent a long period finding all the numbers and ticking them off as she did so.

Trees and bushes provide a wonderful environment for numerous activities involving exploration, mystery, physical challenge, seclusion, wildlife etc.

Heavy rain

Heavy rain, off and on, all week was quite difficult to deal with. On one day, when most children were opting to be inside, they were too excited and noisy and so I insisted that some of the liveliest ones came outside with me. We set about making a shelter. It was quite an experience to sit under the tarpaulin and listen to the rain.

Part of the Creative Cascade set was used by the children to catch the rainwater as it fell off the shelter. Whatever the weather, we keep the garden open. Spare coats, wellies and umbrellas are available – both for the children and the adults!

A dead hedgehog

Today Jacqui, with a group of children, found a dead hedgehog floating in the pond. The children discussed how this could be removed and eventually they succeeded using a long stick and a bucket and then decided it had to be buried. They dug a hole and buried the hedgehog, and then two children went to the woodwork bench and made a cross to stick in the ground. One child then added the word 'hejhog' to the cross. Another child said, 'That cross means "No – do not touch!"' A few days later the children discovered that the hedge-hog had gone. After much discussion, they decided it must have been dug up by a fox.

Overcoming fears

Today Dahir spotted a spider in the classroom and I picked it up. Several children were keen to look, but very few were willing to hold it (The 'Spiderman' film has a lot to answer for!). Dahir and Alex were particularly keen to hold it, but very frightened. They persisted, watching me with the spider crawling all over me. Eventually, after about 20 minutes, they each held it and let it crawl on their hands. Both were delighted with themselves.

> It is wonderful to have the time in a school day to do things like this. To some it may seem like a waste of time. However, who can measure the benefits? These two boys will face future challenges with the knowledge that even when something is frightening, it may be possible to overcome that fear and benefit from a new experience.

Walton-on-the-Naze

The beach trip was a fantastic day. Fifteen children had never been to the beach. Anne, Hanan, Safia, Alisha and Tariq were amazed and couldn't stop laughing all day.

We rope off an area of the water and beach to allow safe supervision.

Parents are obviously anxious about a trip to the beach. We do, in fact, do this trip every year (even though each year the children think it is their idea) and we employ our own lifeguard for the day. I give all the staff a note with instructions and we also discuss the trip the day before we leave. We have one adult to five children. The children are in enclosed areas (bus, park, roped-off beach) and very happy. Once the parents are reassured, every child in the Reception year group comes on the trip.

At school the next day, the children were keen to write about the beach.

There were some lovely collage pictures too – with photos, sand and paint.

We often have extra photos which we store in the graphics area for the children to use in the books and stories that they produce.

The World Cup

The World Cup has meant that flags are flying from many cars and houses. Some children painted flags and these made a lovely display. Jas did the Indian flag on one side and the Greek flag on the reverse and explained, 'My Mum's Indian and my Dad's Greek!'

> During this activity we were surprised at the knowledge that some children have relating to their own culture and flags as well as that of other children. This practical activity allowed them to demonstrate their knowledge in a spontaneous and meaningful way.

Fishing

The fishing game (made last year) needed renewing and several children helped make new fish. They added split pins to the laminated fish so that they would be able to catch them with the magnets on the fishing rods.

This is a very simple game to make and yet so valuable. We have added a number to each fish (and corresponding number of dots) and this then becomes a maths game with many levels of difficulty. Some children see how many fish they can catch; others catch one fish and count the dots; others may catch three fish and add the numbers to calculate their score, e.g. $2 + 3 + 1 = 6$.

Programming

Today, some children were playing with the Bee Bot robot and pushing buttons randomly. Lorna intervened and used the jungle floor puzzle as a mat on which the robot could travel. She then gave instructions such as: 'See if you can make the robot go to the giraffe'.

The children were then estimating distances and changes of direction to move the robot from one animal to another.

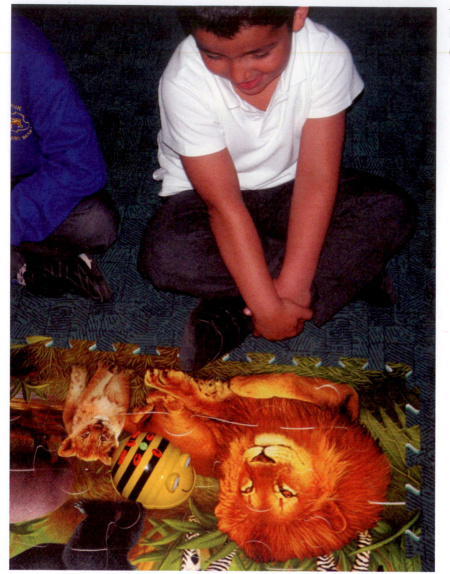

The puzzle is used as a base on which the robot can travel.

Camp fire

On Tuesday the children found a broken piece from a tree, which looked like a tripod. An adult explained how this could be used for hanging a pot over a camp fire. Some children then made a little fire (with sticks and leaves) and then got a big bowl with water and grass etc. to cook on the fire. A large group gathered round, chatting and stirring the pot. Some children started telling ghost stories to each other. After a while, I brought out the guitar and taught them a spooky song and also some traditional camp songs.

There was a lovely calm atmosphere at this activity and the group changed over a period of about 40 minutes, with different children leaving and joining.

Pirates

I am not sure what the trigger was, but there was a sudden interest in pirates this week. This gradually escalated into numerous different activities.

A tiny pirate island.

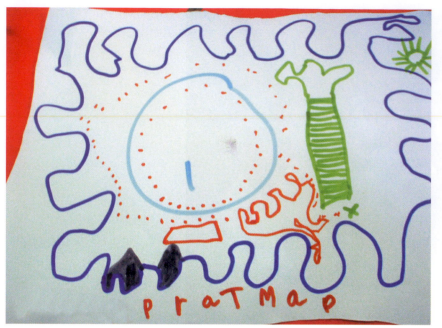

PraTMap = pirate map.

Weighing the dolls

The dolls were looking a bit grubby and Deniz wanted to bath them. When the bathing was finished, Alisha found the large balance and started to compare the dolls to see which was heaviest. Then another group of children tried to find objects to balance against one of the dolls.

As with many activities, there was no adult involvement in this balancing work. The children are keen to experiment and set themselves the questions and challenges.

Activities this month covered many aspects of problem-solving, number and reasoning – all through activities that were initiated by the children and valuable to them. There was no need for meaningless worksheets and no need to 'nag' the children – they got on with the engaging task of playing – the maths was just part of this. This has to be the best way for all learning to occur.

11 July

In July, the focus is again split between the current year and the next. The transition work is explained below. We also complete assessments of the current year group and pass information on as required. In the environment section, I will describe briefly our end-of-year tasks. The diary section shows how the children continue to explore and learn right up until the last day of term.

JULY: TO DO LIST

- Year 1 staff spend time in Reception class.
- Reception children play in the Year 1 classroom.
- Meet with nursery and Year 1 teachers to discuss children.
- Finalise assessments and pass to relevant people.
- Update individual folders.
- Complete final cycle of focus groups, parents' meetings and reports.
- Check, clean, rearrange and order resources as necessary.

Transition work in July

The children in the current Reception class are **familiar with the Year 1 staff** since Year 1 joins us in the playground and garden for the first session most days. If there are any new staff joining the Year 1 team, we ensure that they spend time in the Reception class. The children also get the chance to **play in their new classroom** for at least one session during this month.

    Staff from both year groups meet and discuss each child to point out strengths and any concerns as well as to hand over any confidential information. In our school, a meeting takes place between nursery and Reception staff, as well as between Reception and Year 1 staff.

> For at least the first term in Year 1, the class is run in exactly the same way as the Reception class. Therefore, even though the children are in a new room with new staff, they continue to pursue their own interests supported by the staff.

This year saw extremely smooth transitions – both into Reception and into Year 1. The children in both year groups settled quickly, with very few exceptions. This is the best evidence that our transition work is successful.

Packing away the environment

The end of the year is another important time for reflection and evaluation of the provision. It is a chance to clear out anything that is damaged, rearrange areas that have not been effective, wash equipment, sort through storage areas, stock-take and order new equipment if possible.

This year, for example, we decided to set up a **permanent music area outdoors,** so that we didn't have to keep getting the instruments out of the garage. Lorna set up shelving, with a tarpaulin cover, where the instruments could be stored and tied pots, pans and utensils to the fence nearby to provide more options. This will be developed further in September.

Diary extracts: examples of development and learning

WHAT TO LOOK OUT FOR

- Teachers feel well informed about their new classes (Reception and Year 1).
- Reception children are looking forward to moving into Year 1.
- Final assessments show some leaps in development during last few weeks.
- The environment is ready for the new year.

The examples below are just a tiny sample of the learning that continued right up until the end of term.

Active learning

Jacqui decided that she would like to use a second Butler sink as another pond. The challenge was to move it into position! The children were very keen to help, but it was far too heavy to lift. We decided to roll it along on some round wooden posts that we had. The children were intrigued, and although we could not risk their toes getting squashed, they were able to help by putting the posts into position ahead of the sink – active learning at its best!

The children are often involved in tasks in the class or garden – clearing the leaves, spreading the woodchip, decorating the caravan etc. Such work always involves discussions and challenges so that the learning and development continues and the jobs get done too.

Puppets

The craft books are still popular. This week Lejdina and Lia wanted to make puppets. They asked Ana to help them by holding the fabric while they did the stitches and by cutting a few of the more difficult pieces of fabric (for the eyes). They were delighted with the results and then wrote a story (with an adult scribing parts of it), which the puppets acted out at the end of the day.

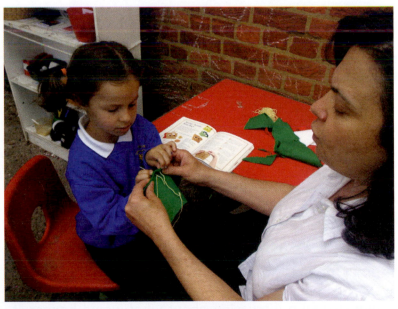

Children often have ambitious ideas like this. However, they completed the task independently, except for cutting the eye shapes. They were insistent that the eyes looked right and the adult support allowed them to be successful.

A cinema

A group of children worked together for a long period to make this 'cinema' and were thrilled when an adult offered to put a real film on the whiteboard.

The model 'cinema' is just visible at the bottom of this photo.

Tigers

A group of boys had been listening to the story tape of 'The Tiger who Came to Tea' and were then playing 'tigers' in the jungle. Jacqui offered to paint their faces, and then the group started a discussion about what would happen if you had a tiger as a pet. Jacqui then got out the book 'Dear Zoo', and when the boys realised there was no tiger in the story, they were keen to make a new page. However, they wanted four very special tigers on the page!

The writing for this page was done by one of the boys who had not opted to write very often (with a little help from Jacqui when he got tired). Although some of the letter formation needs improvement, his phonic ability is clear and he definitely sees himself as a writer. 'He's perfect! We'll keep him!'

The children finished the year as they began – pursuing their own interests, supported by caring adults in an enabling environment. They see school as a wonderful, enabling and exciting place to be. This should be the entitlement of all children.

Conclusion

The children who started in the Reception class at De Bohun in September 2009 had a wonderful year, with numerous experiences they will never forget. All but three of them achieved above-national expectations in their personal, social and emotional development. They learnt to communicate, negotiate and manage their own behaviour within agreed rules and boundaries. They have become confident, independent learners, ready to take on new challenges, and are still excited about school.

Over half the class achieved above-national expectations in all areas of learning. So what did they do in that year? They spent the year pursuing their own interests, supported by enthusiastic, caring adults in an enabling environment. At the time of preparing the revised edition of this book, the children featured in the book have just completed their Key Stage 1 SATS. 86 per cent of these children achieved at, or above, national expectations in reading, writing and mathematics.

Children learn best when they are able to pursue their own interests. A simple idea, but hugely complex to put into practice, as this book has tried to show.

In order for a child to be able to pursue their own interests, they need to arrive at the setting in a comfortable state, both emotionally and physically. The setting needs to be able to support them in this state. If this does not happen, the child may not achieve its full potential, regardless of the quality of the environment, staff or resources. The flower diagram below summarises the prerequisites that allow a child to be in this comfortable state and if any one 'petal' is missing, success will be more difficult to achieve.

Once the children are in the setting, ready to pursue their own interests, there are further prerequisites that the setting needs to have in place in order to succeed. These are summarised on the flower diagram below, and here, too, the system will not be as success-ful if any one 'petal' is missing.

This book describes every aspect of running a successful Reception class where the children pursue their own interests. These systems have been used in nurseries, preschools and in some Year 1 classes. Our work has been scrutinised by parents, students, teachers, advisers and inspectors. But it is the children, who have made such dramatic progress, that are our best evidence of success.

In conclusion, I would like to quote a parent who had serious reservations about our school when his daughter first joined the class. However, as time went on and his daughter flourished, he became one of our strongest advocates:

Our five-year-old has mastered reading, writing and numbers, and created a new social surrounding. She did it completely stress-free, just by playing, following her heart and her interests... the school's method works.

Appendix A: Cake recipe book

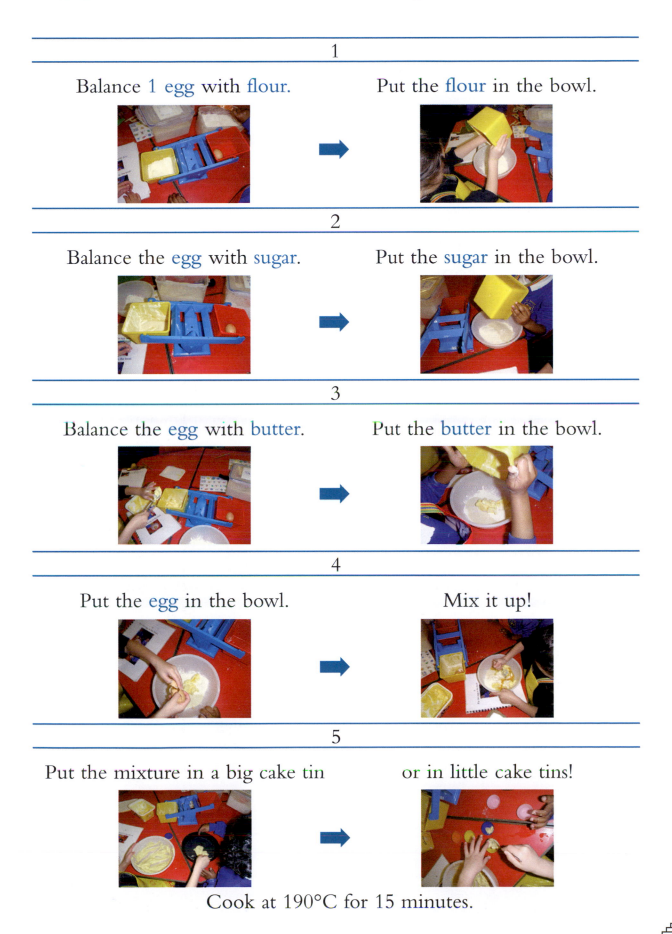

1

Balance 1 egg with flour.

Put the flour in the bowl.

2

Balance the egg with sugar.

Put the sugar in the bowl.

3

Balance the egg with butter.

Put the butter in the bowl.

4

Put the egg in the bowl.

Mix it up!

5

Put the mixture in a big cake tin

or in little cake tins!

Cook at 190°C for 15 minutes.

Appendix B: Playdough recipe

You need:

1 cup of salt
2 cups of plain flour
4 teaspoons of cream of tartar
2 tablespoons of cooking oil
2 cups of boiling water
Food colouring
Large bowl

Mix all the ingredients in a large bowl.

If you keep the dough in a plastic bag or an airtight container, it will last about six weeks.

Appendix C: Planning sheets

Spontaneous planning

	PRIME AREAS			SPECIFIC AREAS			
	C&L	PHD	PSE	LIT	MATHS	UW	EXP A&D
Areas covered:							

W/C: Term: Week:

Focus children: *   *   *

Monday	Tuesday	Wednesday	Thursday	Friday

	Observation	Outome/Activity	Next Steps/Completed
1			
2			
3			
4			
5			
6			

Photo Gallery

Learning journey for .... Term .... Date .... Week ....

	COMMUNICATION AND LANGUAGE	PHYSICAL DEVELOPMENT	PERSONAL, SOCIAL AND EMOTIONAL DEVELOPMENT	LITERACY	MATHEMATICS	UNDERSTANDING THE WORLD	EXPRESSIVE ARTS AND DESIGN	Obs indoors	Obs outdoors	Parent consultation
P R I M E										
S P E C I F I C										

Identified areas for future focus:

General/parents:

Profile:

     *   *   *

Identified areas for focus:

General/parents:

Profile:

     *   *   *

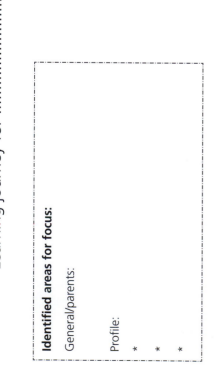

Bibliography

Athey, C. (1990) *Extending Thought in Young Children: A Parent–Teacher Partnership*. London: Paul Chapman Publishing.

Bilton, H. (2010) *Outdoor Learning in the Early Years*. Abingdon: Routledge.

Bowlby, J. (1997) *Attachment and Loss*. London: Pimlico.

Brooker, L. (2002) *Starting School*. Oxford: Oxford University Press.

Bruce, T. (2001) *Learning through Play: Babies, Toddlers and the Foundation Years*. London: Hodder Arnold.

Bruce, T. (2005) *Early Childhood Education*, 3rd edn. London: Hodder and Stoughton.

DfES (2007) *Early Years Foundation Stage Profile*. Nottingham: DfES Pulications.

DfES (2004) *Effective Provision of Pre-School Education* (EPPE). London: Department for Education and Skills/Department for Business Innovation and Skills.

Fisher, J. (2002) *Starting from the Child*, 2nd edn. Maidenhead: Open University Press.

Gerhardt, S. (2004) *Why Love Matters*. Hove: Routledge.

Gussin-Paley, V. (1991) *The Boy Who Would Be a Helicopter*. Boston, MA: Harvard University Press.

HM Government (2000) *Early Years Learning*. POST Report 140. June.

Isaacs, S. (1929) *The Nursery Years*. London: Routledge and Kegan Paul.

Isaacs, S. (1966) *Intellectual Growth in Young Children*. New York, NY: Shockern Books.

Laevers, F. (1994) *Five Levels of Well-being*. Leuven University Press.

Nutbrown, C. (2006) *Threads of Thinking*, 3rd edn. London: Sage.

Read, V. and Hughes, A. (2009) *Developing Attachment in Early Years Settings*. Abingdon: David Fulton Publishers.

Robinson, D. and Groves, J. (2002) *Introducing Bertrand Russell*. Cambridge: Icon Books.

Russell, D. (1932) *In Defence of Children*. London: Hamish Hamilton.

Vygotsky, L. S. (1987) *Mind in Society*. Boston, MA: Harvard University Press.

Whalley, M. (2007) *Involving Parents in their Children's Learning*, 2nd edn. London: Paul Chapman Publishing.

Suppliers

Skips, ditches, charity shops etc.

Parents – great suppliers of 'junk modelling' resources etc.

DIY stores – for ropes, marine plywood, pulleys, woodwork tools and elasticated rope.

www.communityplaythings.co.uk – for wooden blocks (various sizes) and storage units.

www.costco.co.uk – for heavy-duty tarpaulins and shelving.

www.creativecascade.co.uk – for Creative Cascade sets, welly storage and Funky Fountains.

www.ikea.co.uk – for storage units, canopies and children's furniture.

www.impbins.com – for salt bins.

www.olympicgymnasium.com – for A-Frames and ladders, etc. Look in their 'nursery' section.

www.pvc-strip.co.uk – for plastic strips to hang in doorways.

www.shedstore.co.uk – for sheds (Larchlap Overlap Maxi Wallstore 63 is useful for storing large wooden blocks).

www.tooled-up.com – for Sealey woodwork bench, 1.52m (cut the legs down to child height).

www.tts-group.co.uk – for purple sand, clay faces, storage units, toy cement-mixer and Bee Bot.

Consultancy/training

www.freedomtolearn.co.uk – for consultancy and INSET training based on spontaneous planning and child-led learning.

Index

adults' roles in teaching and learning 61–3
animals, interaction with 27–8, 76–7, 130
art work 23–4, 126
attachment disorder 78–9

bridge construction 42–3

carpet sessions 93
Christmas cards and trees 59
computer use 107
conflict resolution 13
construction materials 40–3
cooking 29, 33, 114–15, 145
cued articulation 69
cultural differences and cultural awareness 56, 74, 102, 127, 132
culture of a class 47

dancing 29–30, 44–5, 73–4, 98, 102

focus children 15–19, 113
full-time schooling, readiness for 11

graphics provision 35–39
ground rules 5, 13
Gussin Paley, Vivian 49

home visits 8–10, 32, 113, 124

induction 10–11
interactive whiteboards 107
involvement, levels of 35
Isaacs, Susan 3

key workers 78

Laevers, Ferre 36
language skills 49–50, 69
'learning journeys' 15–19
Literacy Hour 1–2
lunchtime organisation 11–12, 35

mathematical concepts 52–4
music, use of 30, 108, 119

outings 27–8, 63–4, 130–1

parental involvement 15–17, 105–6, 113–14
peer group support 98
phonics teaching 68–70, 91–2, 111, 120
photos of children's homes and families 10, 15–17, 29–30
planning sheets 16, 147–8
play as distinct from work 92
playdough, recipe for 146

reading and reading schemes 21–3, 58, 84–5
reference books 75
risk assessment 63–4, 73
role play 79–80, 90, 95, 103, 109

sand play 25–6, 64, 125
senior management team, support from 91
staff meetings 137
start of the school year 4–5, 8, 10
story scribing 49–51

transition to and from the Reception class 137

uninterrupted play 11

water-based activities 81, 106, 125–6, 129
weapon play 35–6
whole-class teaching 11
woodwork 14, 54, 99, 104
worry dolls 83–4
writing 50–1, 60, 87, 90, 92, 100, 102, 111–12, 120